ANGLING THE INNER BANKS

An Ecosystemic Approach

by Peter Boettger

Published by Warren Publishing

Charlotte, NC
www.warrenpublishing.net

ISBN: 978-0-9853094-9-7
ISBN: 978-1-7323362-0-9

Library of Congress Control Number: 2012950291

Printed in the United States of America

For Marc and Joey

"Great are the works of the Lord;
they are pondered by all who delight in them."

–PSALMS 111:2, NIV

CONTENTS

❖ ❖ ❖

ACKNOWLEDGMENTS

❖ ❖ ❖

Cover photo © Steve Uzzell (www.steveuzzell.com),
courtesy of River Dunes (www.riverdunes.com)

Map of Western Pamlico by Maximum Design
(www.maximumdesign.com), courtesy of River Dunes

www.soundrivers.org

Sound Rivers is a private nonprofit organization that guards the health and natural beauty of the Neuse and Tar-Pamlico River Basins. We partner with concerned citizens to monitor, protect, restore, and preserve the watersheds covering 23% of North Carolina's land mass. Our goal is to provide clean water to our communities for consumption, recreation, nature preservation, and agricultural use. Learn more at www.soundrivers.org.

Because of his appreciation for the Inner Banks resource and respect for the work of Sound Rivers, ten percent of the retail proceeds from this book will be donated to Sound Rivers.

www.machatours.com

At Machapunga Ecotours the goal is to educate people about the natural resources and ecology of our estuaries in a fun, interactive, hands-on way, and to promote the Pungo River/Pamlico Sound region in a sustainable manor.

*"Three-fourths of the Earth's surface is water, and
one-fourth is land. It is quite clear that the good
Lord intended us to spend triple the amount of
time fishing as taking care of the lawn."*
—CHUCK CLARK

INTRODUCTION

❖ ❖ ❖

This book is written to give the reader who is entirely new to
fishing, or an experienced fisherman who is new to the region,
a basic primer for fishing the Inner Banks of the Pamlico
Sound. Because of its unique physical environment, the Inner Banks
present a special set of challenges, as well as opportunities, for
recreational fishermen. Most of all, it is about adapting to constant
change across short spans of time and space.

Deservedly, much has been written about fishing the spectacular
vistas of the North Carolina Outer Banks to the east and the
Chesapeake Bay to the north. The Inner Banks is less celebrated
and its features are comparatively understated, its mystique both
indefinable and alluring. Its hook and line fishing prospects
are abundant, but success does not necessarily correlate with
conformity to well-known convention. Low magnitude tidal forces,
the infrequency of well-defined channels, and rapidly fluctuating
salinity create seemingly erratic conditions when compared to the
predictable rhythms seen in the tidewater regions of the middle and
southeast Atlantic coast. However, recognizable patterns do exist
and the rules of the game change accordingly.

The Pamlico supports a broad diversity of species for the fisherman
to pursue. Its latitude and proximity to the gulf stream put it at a
crossroads, where the seasonal ranges of primarily northern and
southern species overlap. Large sources of freshwater input in the
western portion can effect dramatic changes in salinity, which can
sometimes occur over short distances. Thus, certain combinations
of salinity and temperature variation are capable of hosting a

remarkable array of freshwater, saltwater, and anadromous fishes within surprisingly close proximity to one another.

The Inner Banks is generally recognized as comprising a catchment covering the fresher Albemarle sound to the north and the saltier Core sound to the south. For purposes of this book the Inner Banks shall be defined as the waters of the western Pamlico, west of a line drawn between the southeastern edge of Swan Quarter Bay and the northwestern tip of Carteret County, just east of the Neuse River (See fig. 1). It will include the Pungo River south of Leechville, the Pamlico River east of Washington, the Bay River up to Bayboro, and the Neuse River below New Bern. Many of the techniques described here are also used in the more eastern portions of the Pamlico, where environmental conditions and patterns of fish activity become more consistent as the inlets to the Atlantic are approached.

The species discussed in these pages are considered primarily saltwater, and with the exception of tarpon are most commonly sought after for their combined qualities of table fare, sport, aesthetic attraction, and accessibility for the fisherman of average means. The myriad convolutions of shoreline in the creeks, rivers, and bays avail a generous amount of protected water for safe small boat fishing. A twelve to fourteen-foot jon boat is sufficient for productively fishing these places when launch facilities are nearby. However, to reach some of these areas a more substantial vessel is often needed for traversing vast stretches of open water.

There are far more ways to proficiently catch each species than those described in this book. A few basic techniques will land any of them at given times and places, each one requiring further specialization for consistent success. There are as many variations as there are fishermen, and most of them will develop their own catalogue of successful strategies. Like the people who know it best, the Inner Banks does not give up its secrets easily. Spending time on the water or "paying your dues" will always remain the most important prerequisite for fishing it with skill. Beyond that, this book can offer only an educated guess.

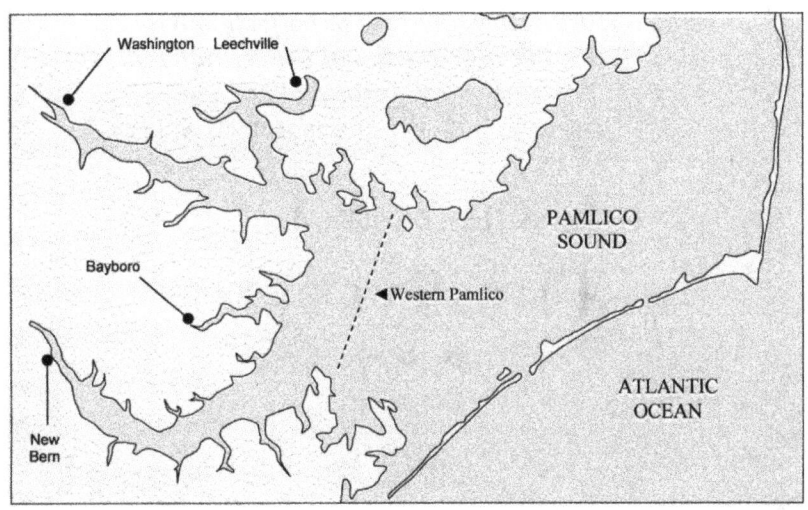

Figure 1: Map of the Western Pamlico

*"Even on the biological level life is not like a
river but like a tree. It does not move toward
unity but away from it and the creatures grow
further apart as they increase in perfection. Good,
as it ripens, becomes continually more different
not only from evil but from other good."*
—FROM *THE GREAT DIVORCE*, BY C.S. LEWIS

CHAPTER 1

THE SYSTEM

❖ ❖ ❖

An estuary can be defined as a semi-enclosed coastal body of
water which has a free connection with the open sea and
within which sea water is measurably diluted with fresh
water derived from land drainage. The Pamlico Sound and its
tributaries are a system of estuaries and sub-estuaries. A multitude
of "drowned" rivers and creeks, characterized by often poorly
defined channels and broad flood plains, converge to form the
sound. The sound itself is best described as more of a lagoon type
estuary, hemmed in by the Outer Banks, with limited tidal exchange
through a few small inlets. It is likely less than 5,000 years old, and
represents a period of peak sea level since the last ice age.

A key characteristic of the Pamlico is its complex pattern of
water circulation. The slope of the coastal plain is very gradual, thus
generating only a slight gravitational contribution to current moving
downstream. The two major drowned river estuaries that contribute
freshwater, the Pamlico and the Neuse, are oversized for the amount
of water they carry, resulting in slow freshwater inflow. It has been
shown that the average transit time for water to reach the Pamlico
Sound from New Bern is one month. Because of its distance from
the inlets, there is little tidal range in the western Pamlico, which
is typically dampened to four inches or less. Movement of water is
actually dominated by wind driven currents.

The prevailing winds are from the south or southwest in spring and summer, and from the north or northwest in fall and winter. Any easterly wind will tend to pile up water along the western edge of the sound, just as west winds will lower the water. A northeast wind will raise the water level dramatically in the Neuse River, but will simultaneously cause a net gain of water in the Pungo, although in the Pungo it would appear on the surface that water is being pushed downstream. These changes can occur on the magnitude of inches or feet and over periods of minutes or days, depending on the intensity and duration of a given wind. A sudden blast of westerly wind in late winter may rapidly expose broad flats that are normally under one to two feet of water. After the front has passed through, the water may return almost as quickly. Conversely, a prolonged period of wet weather combined with a predominance of easterly winds may result in an extended period of unusually high water for days or weeks. Perhaps even more important than higher water, an easterly pattern of wind will produce a rise in salinity, as saltier water from the eastern Pamlico is pushed west.

Salinity is critical in determining the presence or absence of various fishes, as well as their prey species. For example, the low salinity levels during a year with large rainfall amounts may spell a scarcity of mature menhaden, a dietary staple for most predatory fish of the region. Salt levels in the western Pamlico generally range between 5 and 20 parts per thousand (ppt), which is considered brackish. Salinity above 20 ppt is classified as saltwater and below 5 ppt is fresh water. In a typical year, salinity is lowest during the heavier precipitation of late winter through early summer and highest in the drier months of late summer through early winter. Saltier water is heavier than freshwater and sinks to the deeper portions of the water column, where it forms a "wedge" or "lens", which moves upstream and downstream relative to freshwater input and winds (See fig. 2). Jellyfish are a simple barometer for salinity and will be found in fewer numbers as the water becomes fresher.

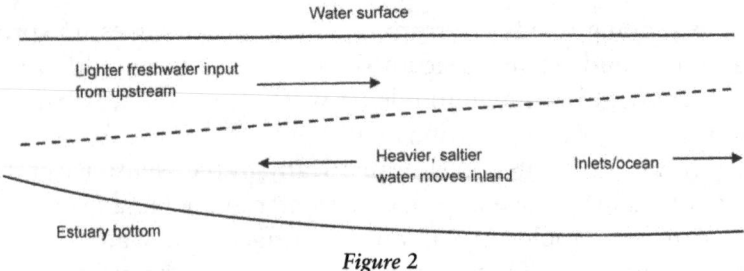

Figure 2

The majority of bottom sediments in the Pamlico estuarine system are medium to fine grain sands and mud, with sand dominating in the eastern portions. Mud composed of fine silts and clays is more common in the open sound, the river channels and mouths, and the tributary creeks of the western Pamlico. Some easily recognizable shoreline plant species are often associated with different bottom types (see Appendix A). For example, the bottom in front of a stand of trees at the water's edge is usually sandy and firm, and typically found along broad, shallow flats at the mouth of a tributary creek or along the banks of a major river. The presence of partially or fully submerged tree stumps, root systems, and fallen logs in these areas are attractive to fish, providing both ambush points and protection from predation. Low *spartina* marsh grasses can also be seen intermingled with trees and shrub species, found in broad expanses near shallow sand flats in high saline areas. Moving upstream into the narrower, lower salinity reaches of the rivers and creeks, black needle rush (*juncus*) becomes more prominent on the banks, and the stream bottom progressively softer and muddier.

As it is today, the Pamlico and its tributaries are subject to a high level of bottom disturbance, meaning that the fine grain sediments of the shallow bottom are vulnerable to wave action and easily stirred up into the water column. Thus, a strong wind can degrade water clarity quite rapidly, sometimes in a matter of minutes in shallow areas exposed to the wind. Pockets of water protected by a lee shoreline will retain clarity temporarily, but a sustained wind disturbance combined with upland runoff of silt during and after rainfall, as well as shoreline erosion associated with wave action, may muddy the entire system and take days of mild weather to clear. Even when calm and clear, the waters of the rivers and creeks are tinted amber by the tannins and lignin of decomposing plant matter released from adjacent flooded swamps and marshes.

Oysters (see Chapter 10), wetland plants (see Appendix A), and menhaden (see Chapter 11) together play a critical role in filtering nutrient pollutants, such as nitrogen and phosphate compounds. Runoff from nonpoint sources such as farms, heavily fertilized golf courses, and suburban lawns loads nitrogen and phosphorus into coastal waters. Excessive nitrogen and phosphorus stimulate the growth of algal blooms that block sunlight and inhibit growth of oxygen producing bottom vegetation. The blooms eventually sink to the estuary bottom, where they are decomposed by bacteria that further consume oxygen from the water, leaving "dead zones" where fish and other creatures cannot survive (see fig. 3).

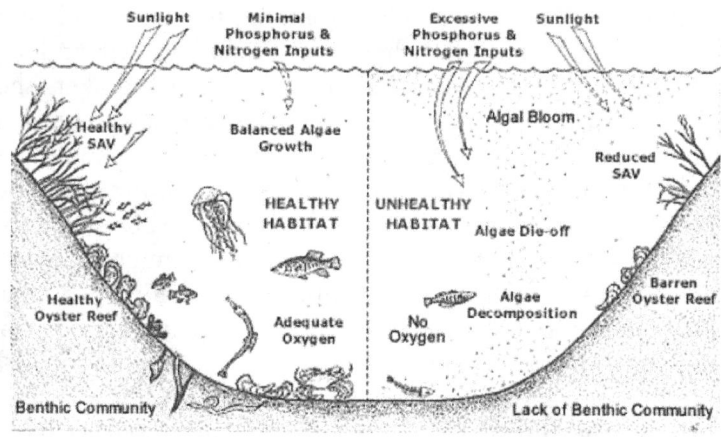

Figure 3: Balanced vs Excessive Nutrients in the Estuary

Estuarine wetlands filter and absorb pollutants, reduce shoreline erosion, recharge groundwater supplies, and serve as primary spawning and nursery areas for resident and migratory finfish. Their metabolism of excessive nitrogen and other nutrient pollutants prevents algal blooms and helps maintain oxygen levels in the estuary as a whole. They capture and sequester a large amount of carbon that otherwise might escape into the atmosphere.

There are two other essential fish habitats in the western Pamlico that play a vital role in maintaining its overall health. Areas of submerged aquatic vegetation (SAV) are otherwise known as "weed" or "grass" beds (see Chapter 12). The physical structure of SAVs increases water clarity by slowing the rate of water flow and modifying wave action, allowing the settling of sediments and food particles. The root system may also help to stabilize the sediment, creating a zone of clear water around SAV beds that allows them to grow and expand. A large number of fish, invertebrates, shellfish, and waterfowl depend on SAVs in various stages of their life cycles for food, shelter from predation, predation on other species, and spawning grounds.

Like SAVs, oysters provide excellent habitat for a variety of fish and crustaceans, and perform an important function in maintaining water quality when present in sufficient numbers. Restored and natural oyster reefs in the Neuse river and Pamlico sound are known to attract large numbers of clams, worms, and shrimp. In turn, the reef community provides abundant foraging for commercially and recreationally important finfish species including red and black drum, spot, gray trout, speckled trout, flounder, croaker, sheep-head, Spanish mackerel, and blue crabs that utilize the reefs. The filter feeding mechanism of the oysters removes and recycles nutrient pollution and organic material, controlling harmful algae blooms and bacterial contamination, and reducing turbidity. Oyster reefs, or "rocks," can also stabilize shoreline erosion by calming wave action and currents in areas where they are abundant. The implications for the fisherman whose tactics depend on water quality are obvious.

Important prey species of the Inner Banks include striped and white mullet, menhaden, silversides, shad, killifish, glass minnows, and shrimp. The finfish species most frequently used as bait are described in Chapter 11. They are all present in seasonally shifting proportions, and most of them move into freshwater at some point in their lifecycle, generally in the spring for spawning. Some of them may spend their entire lives in freshwater marshes. Others are predominantly found in brackish or saltwater and are good indicators of salinity. For example, there are years when menhaden schools are plentiful in the drier periods of mid-summer, only to be driven out by a prolonged pulse of heavy rainfall. The lures described in this book are not precision imitations, but vaguely designed for shape and movement likely to draw a reflexive strike.

In summary, the Pamlico and other estuaries of the Inner Banks are essentially large nurseries that provide goods and services that are economically and ecologically indispensable. These goods and services are known as "eco-system services" and include a large variety of recreational activities. Some estuarine functions are not obvious to the casual observer, such as groundwater recharge and pollution mitigation, and are difficult to assign monetary value. For the fisherman their value is immeasurable.

"There are definite natural things which cannot be broken down into lesser components. Even if the goal of achieving beauty from simplicity is aesthetically less exciting it may force the mind to acknowledge the simple components that make the complicated beautiful."
—FROM *DE STIJL*, THE WHITE STRIPES

CHAPTER 2
SPECKLED TROUT
Cynoscion nebulosus

❖ ❖ ❖

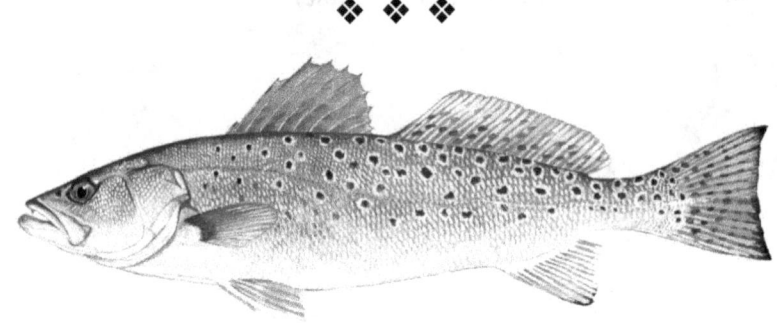

Speckled trout are perhaps the most pursued species by recreational fisherman along the Inner Banks. Truly a magnificent fish, they are of stunning appearance, refined in their behavior, and exquisitely edible. They range from New York to south Florida and the entire Gulf of Mexico, and may grow to a stout sixteen pounds. Coloration is dark gray above, with a bluish gray to olive green iridescence when fresh from the water, and silvery to white below. Well defined black spots are scattered on the dorsal and caudal fins, into the tail fin. There lies the easiest distinction from the gray trout, whose spots do not extend onto the fins. Two prominent canine teeth in the front of the upper jaw command respect when removing a hook.

Trout are particularly sensitive to salinity, and ideally inhabit waters greater than 20 ppt. Thankfully, they are present in good numbers at much lower levels in the western Pamlico, but are noticeably less prevalent at less than 10 ppt, and usually absent at less than 5 ppt.

The population in the western Pamlico is largely made up of smaller young adults and juveniles, although more mature local trout and older visitors from the ocean can be mixed in. A three to six-pound fish is considered a dandy, but an occasional eight to nine-pound whopper is caught. Seasonally, trout spend winter where they can find deep water in the upper creeks, then begin to move downstream when the water begins to warm in early spring. In the Pamlico Sound and its tributaries, trout spawn repeatedly from May into October, peaking in June. The majority of both sexes will have reached sexual maturity before the first year of age, at as small as nine inches. A typical yearling will be twelve to fourteen inches in length, and a healthy female will weigh four pounds by the age of three.

Casting or trolling artificial baits is the most common method for speckled trout fishing in the western Pamlico. The key is to go light, slow, and tight. Six to seven-foot, light to medium action rods rigged with six to ten-pound test line on small diameter reels to allow a slow retrieve are in order. Braided line has several advantages over monofilament. It is much stronger and lighter per unit of diameter and weight, compared to monofilament. For example, most ten-pound test braided line will have approximately the weight and diameter of four-pound test monofilament. Being thinner and lighter, it increases casting distance. It is also less elastic, with less stretch, and is therefore more sensitive to feel and allows a more efficient hook set. However, due to being much softer and having almost no memory, braided line can be extremely difficult to untangle when accidental knots occur. It is much more expensive than traditional monofilament, making tangles even less welcome. Lastly, braided line is more visible in the water. Trout are thought to have keen eyesight, and many trout enthusiasts insist on at least one to two feet of clear monofilament or fluorocarbon line tied between the main line and bait when fishing with a braided main line. The best knots for connecting the two different lines are the Albright knot, Yucatan knot, and Double Uniknot (see Appendix B).

When fishing for trout, the best retrieve is typically the slowest that can be achieved while simultaneously keeping the line tight and providing a bit of enticing action. That said, it often pays to experiment with speed and exaggeration of action when trying to gauge the mood of the fish on any given day. Although "specks" will hit a wide array of lure styles, the basic bait is a jig head or "lead head" dressed with a soft plastic lure, of which there is an infinite variety to choose from, and may resemble anything from baitfish to worms to shrimp in their shape and movement (see Appendix C). The versatile jig head can also be combined with a bucktail, attached to a spinner, or any combination of the three. The classic technique is to bounce the bait along the bottom or intermittently jerk it through the water column in a series of vertical hops, while using the lightest weight possible, and still be able to feel and control the bait. In shallow water (two to five feet) and light winds, a $^1/_8$ oz lead head may be ideal. Deeper water, the presence of current, and stronger winds will likely require a $^1/_4$-$^3/_8$ oz head. Why as light as possible? More often than not, a fish will strike on the drop of the lure between bounces or hops. One explanation is that a lighter bait flutters down slowly, showing more action. This may more realistically represent wounded, vulnerable prey, or perhaps simply allows a prolonged opportunity for an easy ambush. When casting across the wind, it may be necessary to lower the rod and work the bait with a more horizontal retrieve action in order to keep the line tight while maintaining control and sensitivity.

Under most circumstances trout are skittish and easily spooked by noise, especially in shallow water, and should be approached as quietly as possible. They tend to lean toward a subtler approach to taking bait. The strike is often tentative, many times a series of soft taps before firmly taking it. Too many trout are lost by prematurely or overzealously setting the hook. Instead, maintain a slight amount of tension for a split second, until pressure and movement from the fish can be felt, then set the hook quickly and firmly.

Hard plastic plugs, known as "twitch baits" (see Appendix C) have become increasingly prevalent among trout fisherman. Some of these lures are designed to sink rapidly when still. Others sink very slowly or "suspend" in the water column. Either way they are very sensitive to any amount of action and can be made to dart erratically or in a regular rhythm, simulating a wounded baitfish. The suspending version, in particular, is less likely to snag on bottom structure, even when retrieved very slowly. A pause interspersed between twitching maneuvers will often draw a strike.

Springtime speck fishing begins to come alive in late March to early April, when the temperatures in the shallows approach the low to mid-fifties during the day, and hit full stride at temperatures from the upper fifties to above sixty. In early spring trout may still be holding in their wintertime deep-water habitat. At that time the confluence of a narrow sun warmed, nutrient rich, bait laden agricultural canal or small creek that drains into the adjacent waters of a deeper creek makes a prime scenario for finding feeding trout. Excellent action can occur around grass beds as the shallows of broader creeks come alive with increasing temperatures toward mid-spring. To avoid fouling a lure in the grass, look for a thick grass bed growing on a shallow ledge and work the outer edge. If the outer edge drops off to about five feet or more, it is the perfect location for trout on the prowl for a careless bait fish. An effective technique for fishing directly over grass, without entanglement, is to suspend a $^1/_8$–$^1/_4$ oz jig head just over the grass with a small conventional snap float. The weight will track deeper, yet can be adjusted below the float so that the lure will ride freely over the weeds, and remain easily visible to fish holding on the bottom. This can be done behind a trolling motor or by casting and retrieving. An alternative to trolling or casting with a float is to tie on a lipped diving plug (see Appendix C) designed to dive and track just below the surface. The obvious advantage of trolling is that a greater area can be efficiently covered until a school of fish is found. On the other hand, the speed and action of retrieving can be adapted to the mood of the fish on a given day or set of conditions through trial and error.

Trout move down into the mouths of the bigger creeks, out along the lower river shores, and into the bays and sound by early to mid-June in a normal year. As a general rule, more trout are in the open, saltier waters further east from May through September. A prominent point of marsh at the mouth of a creek or bay is an ideal spot. Water blown around the point in a "wind rip" may contain bait species, creating a potential feeding opportunity for trout and other game fish. The presence of structure in the water such as old stumps, sunken logs or timbers, pier pilings, or even crab pots is always an added attraction. However, the deep cool upstream holes cannot be discounted in a very dry year, particularly when the salt wedge has crept inland.

As the water temperature warms during the summer, fishing in the shallows is most productive at first light, lasting until the temperature rises into the upper seventies at around mid-morning. The practice of pitching lead heads or twitch baits, depending on the degree of wind or current, to the edge of the marsh and working them back to the boat with a slow bumping or jigging motion is still the common strategy. The offshore side of the boat should be covered also, where many fish may be holding in deeper, cooler water at this time of year. Continue to follow the fish toward deep holes or sloughs nearby as the early shallow bite tapers off, looking for six to ten feet or more of water. These depths may require as much as 3/8 oz of weight to maintain a tight line. Oyster beds in such areas are excellent places to find specks feeding as the day wears on, and may harbor some bigger fish.

A live baitfish, shrimp, small croaker, or spot fished on a Carolina rig (see fig.8, Chapter 3) is an excellent option, particularly in deep water. It can be worked slowly along the bottom or left sitting in a rod holder while casting artificial baits. The chances of encountering a large trout, or perhaps a drum in these circumstances are greater. Therefore, heavier line in the ten to fifteen-pound range may be a wise precaution.

Fishing live or artificial bait below a "popping" cork (see fig. 4a) in either the shallows or holes can also be an effective alternative during the warmer months of summer and early fall. These floats are designed to use noise as an added attraction when natural prey is abundant and trout are feeding on the surface. Any soft plastic or live bait can be tied at varying depths below the cork, usually gauged to sink into the middle third of the water column. Many trout fishermen prefer to use a live shrimp or shrimp imitation lure. To keep shrimp alive and moving, live shrimp should be hooked just behind the eyes, approximately where the hard ridge, called the "horn" begins protruding from the head. Other hooking techniques may provide a more stable hook set (see Chapter 9). After the bait is cast out and allowed to settle, intermittent, sharp jerking of the cork will cause a "pop" sound generated by the concave end of the cork, which is intended to feign the sound of a surface feeding trout. This motion will simultaneously pull the shrimp toward the surface and cause the plastic or brass beads to clack together along the wire axis. In theory, the noise of the beads and the motion of the bait will attract trout by simulating the sound and appearance of shrimp "snapping" on the surface to avoid a predator. A slotted cork (see fig. 4b) eliminates the need for re-tying to adjust for differences in water depth.

Figure 4a: Combination rattling/popping cork

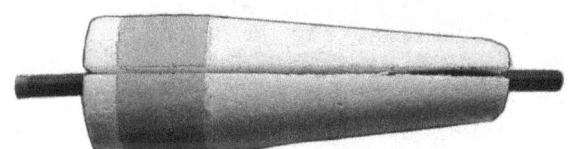

Figure 4b: Slotted cork

Speckled trout will hit "top water" plugs and poppers (see Appendix C) in spring, summer, or fall, but are more likely to do so in the low light of dawn or late evening. An overcast sky may extend the bite throughout the day. Generally, top water fishing for trout should be done quietly and calmly in comparison to the techniques used for the more raucous striped bass (see Chapter 5), and tends to select out the larger trout. The standard retrieve is called "walking the dog" and involves the creation of a zig-zagging pattern on the surface, and is produced by a steady rhythmic twitching of the wrist on the rod hand while reeling slowly. Fine twitches interspersed with occasional pauses are often sufficient to arouse interest while not intimidating the fish.

By late September, when the water temperatures begin to drop into the upper sixties, trout begin to move back into the creek mouths. They feed most aggressively when temperatures are in the upper fifties. A warm autumn can extend the shallow water fishing well into November or December, but when the shallow water temperatures fall below about fifty-five degrees the trend is that the fish move up into progressively deeper water of the larger creeks, where heat is retained further into late fall. Finally, they congregate in the deep, muddy holes of the narrow headwaters for winter, as the temperature drops into the upper forties. There, according to common theory the wind sheltered, tannin stained waters allow the heat of sunlight to be absorbed and held in the dark muck on the bottom. Another probable important factor is the presence of heavier salt water near the bottom, which transfers heat at a significantly slower rate and may extend far upstream to normally fresh waters during a dry year. Such havens are located on the outer portion of a creek bend where sluggish currents have carved out the bank over time, creating a sharp drop-off from the usually shallow opposite shore, and the desirable depth is typically at least six to ten feet. Specks may temporarily move to the nearby warming shallows in the late morning and afternoon, especially during a sustained period of warmer weather.

The technique is "lower and slower" as the water becomes colder. Many devout trout fishermen will work a hard plastic sinking twitch bait or skirted jig head (see Appendix C) slowly and steadily over the bottom, with only an occasional fine twitch, if even that, in these areas. It can be an arduous task to maintain the lure depth just above the bottom, and is easily interrupted by fouling hooks with debris or snagging structure. One way around this problem is to fish with a drop shot rig (see fig. 5), whereby tying a hook onto the main strand of a monofilament or fluorocarbon leader with a Palomar knot allows for an extended tag strand to be left intact for a sinker below the hook. In this case, a soft plastic swim-bait can be fixed on the hook, and worked slowly along just above the sinker. Chances of fouling and snagging the hook are greatly reduced, while the bait is suspended in the strike zone.

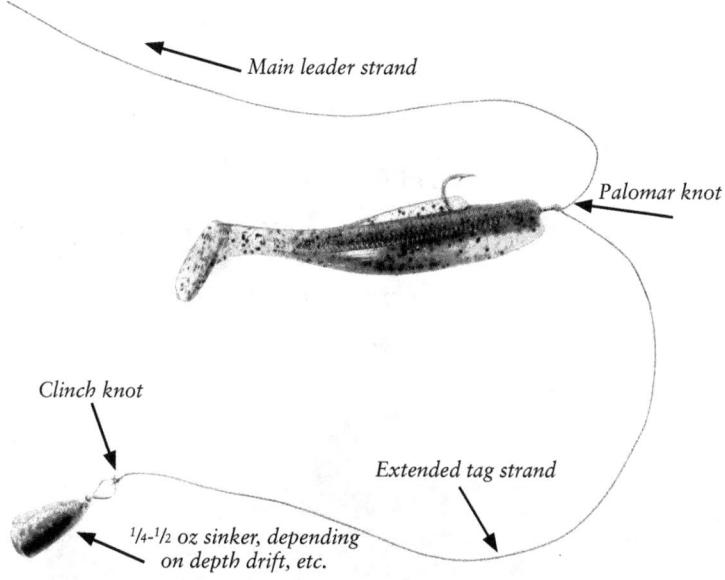

Main leader strand

Palomar knot

Clinch knot

Extended tag strand

$^{1}/_{4}$-$^{1}/_{2}$ oz sinker, depending
on depth drift, etc.

Figure 5: Dropshot rig

"Winterkill" may be the single most devastating cause of mortality for speckled trout in the western Pamlico. Trout start to be adversely affected when the water temperature dips below fifty, and a precipitous decline below forty-five can be lethal, especially for smaller trout. When a strong cold front blasts into the region quickly, many of the trout wintering in the creeks and rivers of the western Pamlico do not have time to escape to the deepest, saltier waters where temperatures are slower to change even under severe conditions. Those who are trapped can literally be seen floating dead or stunned by the thousands. Fortunately, speckled trout reproduce and grow quite prolifically, and the population will rebound in two to three years after such an event.

*"For it is a jubilee and is to be holy for you;
eat only what is taken directly from the fields."*
–LEVITICUS 25: 12

CHAPTER 3
SOUTHERN FLOUNDER
Paralichthys lethostigma

❖ ❖ ❖

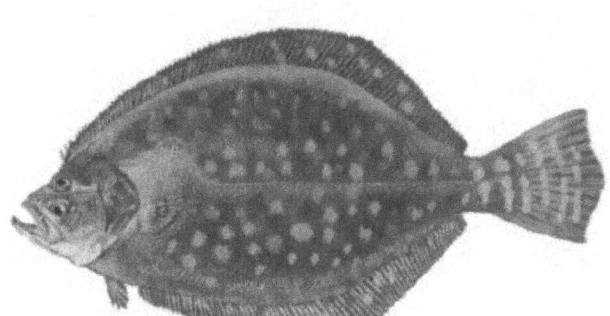

lounder are not only highly prized table fare, but quite possibly
the wiliest of fish to be caught under the conditions occurring in
the Inner Banks. They are illustrative of the species diversity to
be found in these waters. The three subspecies (see fig. 6) that inhabit
the area are southern flounder (*Paralichthys lethostigma*), summer
flounder (*Paralichthys dentatus*), and gulf flounder (*Paralichthys
albiguttata*). Gulf flounder primarily frequent high salinity waters
over sandy bottoms near the inlets from Oregon Inlet to Texas. In
the western Pamlico, only small populations have been recorded in
tributaries around the mouth of the Neuse River, and will not be
discussed here.

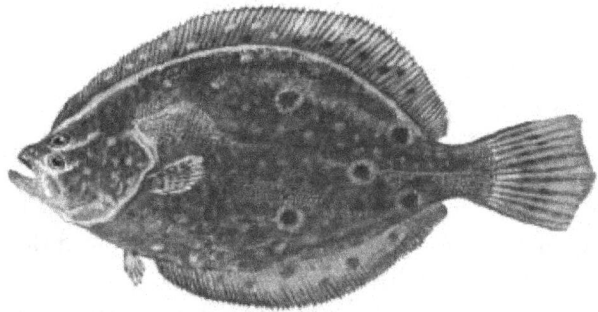

Summer Flounder

Gulf Flounder

Figure 6

Summer flounder are found in estuarine and coastal waters from Nova Scotia to the east coast of southern Florida, but are most abundant from Cape Cod to Cape Hatteras. Rapid hormonal changes allow the coloration on the upper side changes color to match the bottom habitat and varies from drab olive-green to brown or gray, sometimes nearly black on dark sediments. Ocelli are dark spots rounded with a lighter border, resembling an eye, otherwise known as "eyespots". There are usually many eyespots scattered over the upper side, but five are always consistently placed; two near the base of the dorsal fin, two almost directly below them near the anal fin base, and one in the middle on the lateral line. Summer flounder can grow to thirty-seven inches, weighing up to twenty-six pounds.

Southern flounder inhabit riverine, estuarine, and coastal waters from southern Virginia to Texas. Compared to summer flounder, they are relatively slender, with the depth of the body being less than one-half the length, and have larger mouths and larger teeth. There are no eyespots, although they are often spotted and blotched, and females can reach thirty inches in length.

Flounder begin life with one eye on each side of their bodies. When they are larvae the right eye shifts to the left. They may change from male to female as juveniles or young adults depending on environmental, behavioral, and social factors. Both species of flounder tolerate a wide range of salinities well as juveniles and sub-adults, but the majority of summer flounder occur in higher salinity regions and are rarely found in NC estuaries after their second summer, when reaching sexual maturity at about twelve inches in length. The larger adult summer flounder inhabit sandier areas near inlets and along coastal beaches. Southern flounder also achieve sexual maturity by age two, but grow more rapidly, and females are at about fourteen and a half to seventeen inches at that time, males at about ten inches. Males older than three years and longer than thirteen inches have rarely been recorded in Atlantic Coast waters.

Fortunately for fishermen in the western Pamlico, Southern flounder are well suited to low salinity far into adulthood and the females are normally the "keepers" that are caught. Both species move into deeper ocean waters during late fall and winter, and are caught most abundantly in the western Pamlico from April into December. Summer flounder are more likely to aggressively search and pursue their prey, while their southern cousins tend to remain still on the bottom, where they can flex their fins to partially bury themselves in the sediment, while waiting for prey to come within striking distance. No effort is wasted by these curmudgeons, and a grumpy expression of annoyance when boated reflects their great displeasure with having a choice meal rudely interrupted.

Occasionally, during periods of calm in the heat of summer, flounder will participate in a strange phenomenon sometimes known by local people as a "flounder walk" (see fig. 7). Periods of little or no wind during long, hot days and nights allow the still waters to settle into well-defined layers. Under these conditions there is no mixing between the more buoyant, oxygen rich layers of fresher water in the upper water column and the heavier salt wedge at the bottom. A lack of photosynthetic activity, combined with microbial decomposition of decaying organic matter on the bottom, further depletes the oxygen supply to extremely low levels. Such stagnant water can literally drive bottom dwelling flounder, crabs, and other creatures to the shoreline in a desperate effort to find higher levels of oxygen, even attempting to gulp it from the air. The weakened fish are quite docile, appearing to offer themselves with no resistance to those fortunate enough to reap the harvest. Some have described these events as colored with a festive, almost mystical aura. Left alone, the hapless flounder may live to walk another day if they can find enough oxygen, or if a wind adequate to mix the surface and bottom water soon follows.

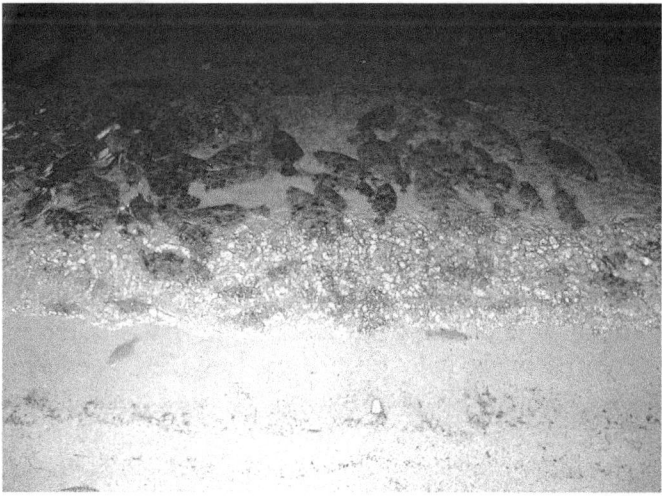

Figure 7: Flounder walk or "jubilee"

Flounder will hold in a variety of places, sometimes for no apparent reason. Conventional areas include holes and channels. A "hole" can be just a subtle depression in comparison to surrounding shallows. During early morning or late evening hours, groups of fish can also be found on sandy bottoms in very close proximity to shore, often grouped within only a few square feet, and may be present in less than a foot of water. Another favorite haunt is a small gut or ditch draining from the marsh. Current is a luxury for the flounder fisherman in the western Pamlico and is ideal for offering the bait at a natural pace, whether drifting with live bait or tossing lures. No matter the scenario, flounder are waiting to ambush moving prey from their position on the bottom, so the bait must be presented to them as deeply as possible, without actually dragging the bottom. In the western Pamlico the majority of flounder caught by the recreational fishermen are a welcome bonus, coincidental to fishing for speckled trout or puppy drum, and are not specifically targeted. However, there exists a smaller portion of anglers who devote concentrated time and special techniques to flounder fishing.

The time honored classic rigging for flounder is the "Carolina rig", which is essentially a modified fish finding rig designed for live bait fishing near the bottom. It consists of sliding an egg sinker onto the line, followed by a barrel swivel tied on below it, and about eighteen inches of leader with a hook tied onto the other end of the barrel swivel (see fig. 8). The genius of the Carolina rig is found in its versatility. It can be cast to shore and reeled back slowly as if working a lure, or can be dragged from a drifting boat. Either way the egg sinker slides along the bottom, while the bait fish is able to swim along a few inches above, exposed and vulnerable to an awaiting flounder. An added benefit is that the smooth contour of the sinker and swimming bait make the entire rig less likely to snag on bottom structure, which can be prevalent in the western Pamlico. In comparison to speckled trout gear, somewhat stouter rods and line are required when fishing Carolina rigs. Ten to twelve pound test line, with twenty to twenty-five-pound test leaders and one half to two ounce egg sinkers are adequate. Of course, adjustments are necessary for depth and possible current, as well as speed of the drift. Another option is to fish two baits, one hooked above the other, with the sinker dragging along the bottom below. Live bait should consist of whatever is available seasonally, mud minnows in the spring and menhaden or finger mullet in summer and fall.

Figure 8: Carolina Rig

Southern flounder are habitually cautious and frequently downright timid when taking bait. For this reason, the speed of the drift or retrieve should err on the side of being too slow. The initial strike may be a dull tap followed by a slightly heavier feeling in the line, or the line may simply go slack. They are notorious for holding the bait in their mouths before ingesting with commitment. As a general rule it is best to wait for a count of at least five to ten seconds before setting the hook. Even then the fish may move toward the boat, not exerting much effort until in close, where it will suddenly begin a vigorous fight. Although often caught in shallow water, flounder are capable of generating a tremendous amount of downward pressure, which combined with violent head shaking can enable them to spit the bait unless firmly hooked. It is best to avoid pulling directly upward on the fish when it is close to the boat. Instead, bring the fish into net range by leading it closer, back and forth at a diagonal angle.

Flounder will readily hit a variety of jigs if presented slowly and in close proximity to the fish, a good technique when an apparent school of flounder has been located. The lure should be fished as though fishing for speckled trout, and again, a pause before setting the hook should ensue after a suspected hit, unless the strike is obvious and aggressive.

Whether fished with live bait or with artificial lures, fishing for flounder in the western Pamlico is typically much different than fishing the deeper and saltier inlets, channels, and tidal creeks of the outer coast. Despite their prevalence they may in their own way be the most challenging species to hook and land. Success demands great patience and self-discipline.

*"Can you pull in the leviathan with a fishhook
or tie down his tongue with a rope? Can you put
a cord through his nose or pierce his jaw with a
hook? Will he keep begging you for mercy?
Will he speak to you with gentle words?"*

–JOB 41:1-3

CHAPTER 4
RED DRUM

Sciaenops ocellatus

❖ ❖ ❖

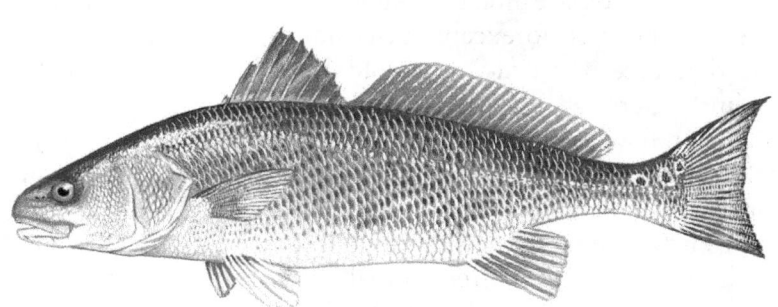

The red drum was officially designated the state saltwater fish of North Carolina in 1971. It thrives in estuarine and coastal waters, extending along the western Atlantic and Gulf coasts from Massachusetts to northern Mexico. This is a fish of many names including "redfish" as it is known in the gulf, "spot tail bass," and "channel bass."

Sciaenops ocellatus literally means "perch-like sea fish with an eyespot." The body is elongated with a large head, and the mouth is located more ventrally behind the tip of the snout. Dorsally, coloration can vary from nearly silver to coppery orange to occasionally black to the more common reddish bronze. The stomach is always white, but by far the most distinguishing feature is at least one large, black eyespot on the upper part of the tail base, which has been said to represent "a little tar on its heel." Although normally located at the base of the tail, the number of spots can range into dozens, distributed anywhere between the head and tail. The absence of a spot altogether is rare.

The Gulf and southern Atlantic coastal states are renowned for large numbers of drum. However, North Carolina fishermen can rightfully take great pride in celebrating the state's legendary reputation for the bigger fish of the species. From Georgia to Texas the state records for red drum range between forty-three and sixty-one pounds, obliterated by the world record ninety-four-pound specimen landed on the beach in Avon, NC, as of this writing. Delaware, Maryland, Virginia, and South Carolina have recorded respectable specimens of seventy-four to eighty-five pounds. Fish over fifty pounds are not uncommon in North Carolina and the western Pamlico is no exception. Drum are a long-lived fish, and some that are over sixty years old have been caught in North Carolina waters.

No matter where they are found, red drum grow at a very fast rate. They reach approximately eleven inches and one pound in their first year, seventeen to twenty-two inches and three and a half pounds in two years, and twenty-two to twenty-four inches and six to eight pounds by year three. Sexual maturity is developed in three to five years, the majority having reached it by age four when they are thirty to thirty-seven inches long. By age five they are at about forty inches, and at that point their rate of growth in length slows abruptly, with proportionately greater gains in weight and girth. For the first three to four years young red drum spend their lives in the sounds and estuaries or in the surf zones near inlets, and can tolerate a wide range of salinities. After maturing they prefer the ocean, only returning to the estuaries to spawn in late summer and early fall, when males attract females by emitting a drumming sound by contracting muscles around the swim bladder.

The larvae are scattered throughout the western sound by wind driven currents, but the majority are carried to the upper reaches of the estuary where they settle in protected, shallow, low-salinity habitats to utilize the abundant food supplies associated with grass beds. Small juvenile red drum leave their shallow water habitat during the extreme cold of winter for deep water areas, then return in spring as water temperatures rise.

North Carolina fishermen have applied a variety of criteria to the definition of "puppy drum", but it generally refers to the younger, sexually immature fish of the species. Those in the three to five year-old classes weighing eight to fifteen pounds are sometimes called "yearlings". To avoid confusion, keep in mind that these terms are used quite loosely in eastern North Carolina fishing circles.

Puppy drum constitute the large majority of red drum taken in the Inner Banks. Like their speckled cousins, they can be caught year-round, but most fish are caught in early spring through late fall. As with most fish species, early morning and late evening are prime times for the puppy drum bite. Time of day becomes less of a factor when large schools gather in autumn to feed ravenously before moving toward the inlets. Puppy drum will strike an assortment of artificial lures, essentially of the same types used for speckled trout, and are predictable cohabitants with trout in areas of varying depth along the shores of the creeks and rivers. Structure in the form of stumps, fallen trees, submerged logs, rocks, and crab pots are a key ingredient for attracting drum to an area. Rough water forcing bait against a windward bank is a likely setting for feeding drum.

The rods, reels, tackle, and techniques used for speckled trout are also very effective for puppy drum. However, when specifically targeting drum a heavier rod, reel, and line are required for bigger and stronger fish. A medium action rod of six to seven feet and a medium sized reel spooled with ten to twelve-pound test line is sufficient for presenting light lures, while providing a bit of back bone during the fight. Compared to trout they are characteristically more assertive in their approach to the bait, affording the angler the luxury of a less disciplined retrieve, and will strike a faster, more exaggerated action with authority. Live or cut bait fished on circle hooks dramatically reduces deep hooking, and can be very effective for puppies and yearlings when fished below a float or on a Carolina rig.

Red drum are not usually seen "tailing" in the western Pamlico like they are on the Gulf coast, and therefore it is generally not a sight fishery. The exception occurs when baitfish are abundant in late summer and early fall when schools of puppy drum or yearlings can be seen in very shallow water, slashing into schools of corralled menhaden and finger mullet within a few feet of shore. If fortunate enough to be in the vicinity of such an event, these fish should be stalked quietly and slowly with a trolling motor, push pole, or by wading. Successfully placing a lure in front of the fish under these circumstances will more than likely result in an aggressive strike.

"Big drum" greater than five years old, aka "old drum", are present in the western Pamlico during the spawn, from roughly late June thru mid-October. The prime fishing is in August and September, when mature adults are schooled in large numbers for the peak of spawning activity. Higher salinity areas near the river mouths or the open sound, featuring water depths of at least ten feet, are the top spots likely to produce the biggest drum. A sharp ledge, dropping from a depth of three to five feet to ten feet or more is ideal, and is enhanced by a brisk wind pushing onto the ledge, thus providing a situation where drum can corral hapless baitfish trapped against the ledge by wind and waves. They can be caught throughout the day and night, but the bite is typically best from just prior to sunset until dawn.

Well planned outings for old drum involve chumming to attract fish and direct feeding into closer proximity. The general idea is to disperse a trail of pungent scent and tasty morsels for hungry fish to follow. Menhaden oil is available in some tackle shops and is a favorite product. It can be infused precisely into the water from an IV-style drip bag at about a drop every five to ten seconds, or released less exactly from dog chow soaked in it overnight and hung overboard, contained in a fine mesh onion bag. More costly mesh pots and bags constructed of anti-corrosion treated wire can be purchased, and frozen chum blocks are also available commercially. Frozen chum blocks contain a blend of fish bodies, fat, blood, and oil. A potent do-it-yourself concoction of local bait fish, crabs, and even shrimp scraps can be mashed up in a sausage grinder. Any small mesh bag or secure plastic container with appropriately sized holes drilled in it will work for allowing the mix to ooze out slowly, as it thaws in the water. Anchor lines make an excellent cable for suspending chum at various depths if so desired.

The more traditional method for catching the larger drum involves heavy spinning or bait-casting reels spooled with at least 200-250 yards of twenty to thirty-pound test line on heavy weight rods are employed when targeting these behemoths. Large circle hooks tied onto conventional bottom and fish finding rigs can be used as terminal tackle, but anglers are encouraged to use a type of bottom rig (see fig. 9) designed specifically to avoid gut hooking and facilitate easy hook removal, thereby greatly reducing mortality of these magnificent fish following the release. A wind-on fifteen to twenty-foot "shock line" consisting of fifty to sixty-pound test monofilament line tied between the bottom rig and the mainline on the reel with a double uni-knot, Yucatan, or Albright knot (see appendix B) avails more leverage as the fish is brought close to the boat, and is safer for handling with bare hands in comparison to thinner braided line.

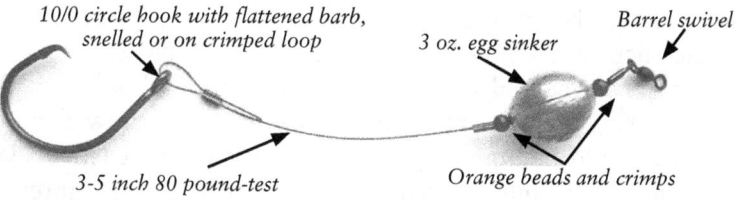

10/0 circle hook with flattened barb, snelled or on crimped loop   3 oz. egg sinker   Barrel swivel

3-5 inch 80 pound-test   Orange beads and crimps

Figure 9

Big drum will take live bait, cut bait, or whole dead baits willingly. They can be enticed with a multitude of offerings including menhaden, mullet, croaker, spot, blue crabs, pin fish, and bluefish. Baits should be checked frequently to ensure freshness, and be replaced when stolen by opportunistic crabs and other small scavengers. No hook set should be necessary when fishing with circle hooks, as the hook is designed to slide to the corner of the fish's jaw and catch as it runs with the bait and the line straightens. Lines should be kept tight by using heavy weights and holding onto rods, rather than leaving them unattended, to minimize any chance of swallowing the hook. If a rod is left unattended, set enough tension to pull the hook into the corner of the jaw immediately, rather than allow the fish to run easily against the drag and swallow the hook. When a rod bends, tighten the drag and begin the fight.

In more recent history anglers have begun adapting the same light tackle methods with artificial lures, previously described for smaller fish, to fishing for the bigger classes of drum. The difference is that it is done with much larger and heavier versions of the baits and rigging. Light in weight, but medium/heavy action, flexible rods from six and a half to seven and a half feet in length allow the fisherman to work the larger lures effectively for prolonged periods. Appropriately matched reels should be spooled with twenty to thirty-pound test braided line for greater casting distance and better lure action. Again, a length of heavier clear monofilament line may desirable as a shock line between the main line and bait, and is normally used below popping corks.

Schools of menhaden are scattered throughout the western Pamlico through the summer and well into fall. Menhaden that are "nervous" reflect a likely presence of drum or other predators nearby, and are tightly grouped and erratically splash in linear patterns on the surface. At times large drum can even be seen crashing the bait at the surface. However, a relatively quiet school of menhaden does not rule out the presence of drum lurking below them. These schools should be approached quietly, but within casting distance. Popping rigs, diving or floating plugs, and top water lures should be worked aggressively through and around the schools of bait to attract attention.

Heavier tackle reduces fight time, leaving the fish in better condition for survival after release. All barbs on hooks should be flattened to facilitate quick removal. Avoid taking fish out of the water to remove hooks whenever possible. If hooked deeply and not amenable to easy removal, cut the line and do not risk further trauma. In cases where a fish must be brought into the boat, guide it into a soft plastic landing net large enough to evenly distribute support for the fish, and lift it gently into the boat. Limit handling and photo time to a minimum, then release the fish by holding it upright in the water until it is clearly reoriented and starts to swim. These simple precautions will help ensure that a healthy population of red drum will thrill North Carolinian fishermen for generations to come.

"If my mother put on a helmet and shoulder pads and a uniform that wasn't the same as the one I was wearing, I'd run over her if she was in my way. And I love my mother."

–BO JACKSON

CHAPTER 5
STRIPED BASS

Morone saxatilis

❖ ❖ ❖

There is nothing restrained about "stripers" (also known as "striped bass", "rock", or "rockfish"). Not known for meekness, nor any sense of deferred gratification, they pursue their wants and needs with reckless abandon. Arguably, the best part of fishing for stripers is in not having to be concerned with delicate sensitivities. They are refreshingly uncomplicated, even in the western Pamlico.

Their appearance is suggestive of a straight forward, linear approach to life. The body is streamlined and silvery in color, shaded olive to blue on the back, and adorned with seven or eight black stripes running parallel on the sides from behind the gills to the base of the tail. Truly anadromous, they spend their adult lives in salt or brackish waters, but spawn in the moving freshwater of the upper watersheds. Stripers are believed to live up to thirty years. The largest on record are two females caught in 1907 with seine nets in the Albemarle, weighing 125 pounds each. In coastal NC they grow to approximately ten to eleven inches during the first year of life, sixteen to seventeen inches at age two, and reach sexual maturity during their third year at twenty to twenty-two inches. Thereafter, yearly growth slows to under two inches per year. Spawning in eastern NC takes place from late March to early June, peaking when water temperatures reach sixty-two to seventy degrees.

The Roanoke/Albemarle, Tar/Pamlico, and Neuse river systems represent the largest populations of spawning stripers in North Carolina, although less significant populations are scattered in coastal rivers further south. It is known that a fraction of older, mature fish in the Roanoke/Albemarle complex migrate into the ocean in winter months. The stripers of the Tar/Pamlico and Neuse systems are thought to be strictly riverine. They spend their adult lives in the lower portion of their respective rivers, for the most part moving upstream to freshwater during the spring spawn. However, isolated numbers of fish hunker down for winter in some of the surprisingly deep holes found in the far upstream reaches of certain creeks and adjoining canals. Genetic analysis has demonstrated the three native populations to be very similar, with the Tar/Pamlico and Roanoke/Albemarle being virtually identical in their genetic diversity. Despite the Tar/Pamlico and Neuse rivers being directly connected by the Pamlico Sound, the Neuse river fish exhibit a significant genetic difference. The possible effect of aggressively stocking these fish in recent years is not known.

When they are hungry stripers are known to attack bait aggressively and often viciously, and are opportunistic in their feeding behavior. Spinner baits and buzz baits (see Appendix C), jigs, spoons, plugs, cut bait on bottom rigs, flies, top water lures, and live baits are all effective for stripers. However, the bait of choice may differ somewhat, dependent on time of year and local conditions.

Striper fishing in the western Pamlico may be prolific at any time from fall through spring, normally less productive in summer. Early spring is thought by many fishermen to be prime striper time in the region. As the days begin to lengthen and surface temperatures are warmed by the sun, stripers arouse from the lethargy of winter in the mood to feed and procreate. The spawn begins up in the creeks, and fishing for stripers at this time utilizes tackle and techniques reminiscent of largemouth bass fishing. Shallow diving lipped plugs, spoons, spinner baits, buzz baits, and jigs cast near shallow water structure or edges of weed beds on light spinning gear or bait casters will draw startling strikes. These fish are not easily intimidated under most circumstances, especially in spring. The pace of retrieve can be fast or slow, requiring no specific pattern of action that must be applied to attract interest.

Sometimes it seems that stripers actually relish a little commotion, and top water lures (see Appendix C) are designed to create it. One of the most common top water plugs used to fish for stripers is the "popper". Poppers float on the surface and are engineered with a concavity on the front which cups air, and will literally emit a popping or gurgling sound when given a quick jerk, by plunging the plug forward into the water and producing a noisy splash. The retrieve may be reeled straight in at various speeds or syncopated with experimental ratios of pause and pop. Some top water plugs feature attached planers pre-set at angles to generate a jittery back and forth motion, prominent wake, and excited splash while they skitter across the water imparting a sense of panic. Buzz baits draw attention with a rotating blade that churns the surface of the water much like an outboard propeller, trailed below by a gaudy plug. Still, others are designed to glide more smoothly on the water, allowing the angler to improvise sharper twists and turns in the retrieve. "Walking the dog" is a popular method of pulling in these lures, where the angler rhythmically twitches the rod, allowing a bit of slack between each twitch, all the while continuing the retrieve at a steady pace, which results in a zig-zag path. Jarring strikes at top water plugs are often preceded by a swirling wake behind the lure, as the fish positions itself for attack. If there appears to be some hesitation, a slight increase in speed, extra twitch, or brief pause may trigger the final assault. A rambunctious strike will sometimes send the plug flying or result in a failed hook-up. In such cases the fish will likely hit again if the fisherman presents another opportunity.

Stripers become sluggish in summer, retreating to deep water structure to escape the heat. At this time of year, a tempting meal of cut or live bait, literally dangled in front of them is sometimes the only means for bringing them to the table. Cut bait suspended near channel bottoms around bridge pilings, bulkheads, and other deep structures can be effective. Lead heads skirted with soft plastic grubs and jigged vertically, deep in the water column, may also draw a response.

Whether using cut bait or jigging, the key is to present the bait as near to structure as possible, making it a temptation too close to refuse.

The return of lower temperatures in autumn stimulates stripers to feed voraciously, and return to the shallows during early morning and late evening hours, which remain the optimal time of day for fishing. Trolling an assortment of lures is an easy, often successful method for hooking fish during the cooler seasons. An added convenience is that it is not necessary to troll for stripers with a quiet electric motor, for they are not spooked by conventional outboards. In early to mid-fall, baits should be trolled through the middle and top thirds of the water column. Trolling speed should be adjusted to the mood of the fish and type of lure. Favored lures include rattling plugs, lipped plugs designed to dive to various depths, and bucktails or jigs dressed with fluttering soft plastics. A light casting outfit should always be kept readily available for sight casting, should fish be spotted working bait.

Stripers are more tolerant of colder water compared to the trout, flounder, and red drum residing in the western Pamlico, and are a cold weather staple for hardier souls willing to brave the elements. They will continue to feed throughout winter, dependent to a large degree on weather trends. Like the other fishes, when late fall becomes early winter stripers descend deeper to lurk just above the bottom. The pace for drawing strikes, whether casting or trolling, becomes slower and strikes less aggressive. Time of day becomes less critical, and in fact a rise in water temperature by only a degree or two toward mid-afternoon is an advantage. Regardless of the time of year, structure is of paramount importance. Baits should be trolled, casted, jigged, or floated over deep water artificial and natural reefs, or in deep water adjacent to bridge pilings and railroad trestles of the lower river channels. In the late dead of a harsh winter, even striped bass must conserve their energy and resources. They can become less aggressive and lures should be worked slowly. In these circumstances a strike may feel like a subtle tap, but the hook should be set immediately. Another technique is to fish a live minnow or jig skirted with soft plastic head deep below a float, moved only by a light to moderate breeze. Lastly, an American Eel fished live from a drifting boat (see chapter 11), is acknowledged among experienced fisherman to be the single best bait for striped bass at any time of year.

*"It was kind of lazy and jolly, laying off
comfortable all day, smoking and fishing,
and no books nor study."*
–FROM *THE ADVENTURES OF
HUCKLEBERRY FINN*, BY MARK TWAIN

CHAPTER 6
WHITE PERCH
Morone americana

Big things come in little packages. Less is best. Keep it simple. Smaller is better. Such might be the slogans that epitomize the white perch and the guiding principles of those who purposely seek out these feisty little fish. Ever adaptable, they tolerate a wide range of temperatures and salinity throughout their native habitat along the east coast from South Carolina to Nova Scotia, and have flourished in many land locked freshwater systems where they have been introduced. In some areas they are considered a pest, due to a ravenous appetite for the eggs of other species considered more desirable, and must not be returned to the water when caught. The white perch fulfills significant ecologic niches as both prey and predator. Despite its sometimes maligned reputation, for its admirers this fish does not take a back seat to anyone, either for sport or as table fare.

White perch are able to live in waters of thirty-two and a half to ninety degrees Fahrenheit. Spawning may take place in resident waters or after migrating long distances to brackish or freshwater for marine populations, generally in waters less than 4.2 ppt. They are reproductively prolific compared to other fish of similar size, lay large quantities of eggs, and can easily outcompete other species and become overpopulated where introduced. During their first year, the juveniles stay close to shore in the creeks and estuaries, just downstream from the spawning areas, until one to one and a half inches in length. Most males and females are sexually mature by two years of age, at three to four inches in length. They may live as long as nine years, reach fifteen inches in length, and usually a little over two pounds in weight. The NC state record fish weighed two pounds and fifteen ounces, and was caught from Falls of the Neuse Reservoir in 2001. An average mature adult measures eight to ten inches long and weighs three quarters to one pound.

White perch in the western Pamlico may be full time residents in its brackish or fresh waters, or might be temporary visitors from the salty waters of the Atlantic. Nevertheless, they are a true anadromous fish and will spawn in the estuary, rivers, creeks, or marshes from late winter into mid-spring. Actually a member of the bass family, white perch are homely in appearance by comparison to their close relative, the Striped Bass (*Morone saxitilis*). Their body is proportionately much deeper and thinner, the head more concave, and the mouth is smaller. Coloration on the dorsal surface occurs in various shades of dark grayish-green, olive, and silvery gray. The sides are pale olive or silvery green, and the belly is silvery white. Large fish of the species often wear a bluish luster on the head.

Fishing for white perch can be excellent at any time of year. Typically gathering in large schools, they are not finicky and will aggressively take a wide variety of baits, both artificial and natural. The general pattern in the western Pamlico is that they congregate further upstream in deeper, freshwater creeks in winter and early spring, but may also hibernate in the deep pools and channels of the rivers and estuary. Deep water structure such as deadfall trees, railroad trestles, and dock/bridge pilings are likely places to find white perch in winter. Natural baits fished down deep on typical bottom rigs (see fig. 10a) with two or more hooks and small bell sinkers slowly drifted from a boat is an effective technique during cooler months. Cut and live bait can also be presented at various depths beneath simple float rigs (see fig. 10b) or suspended in the water with a cane pole. Some twitching or crisp movement of the bait will attract the attention of the fish. Like most fishes, perch are more sluggish and less aggressive in their feeding behavior in the cold.

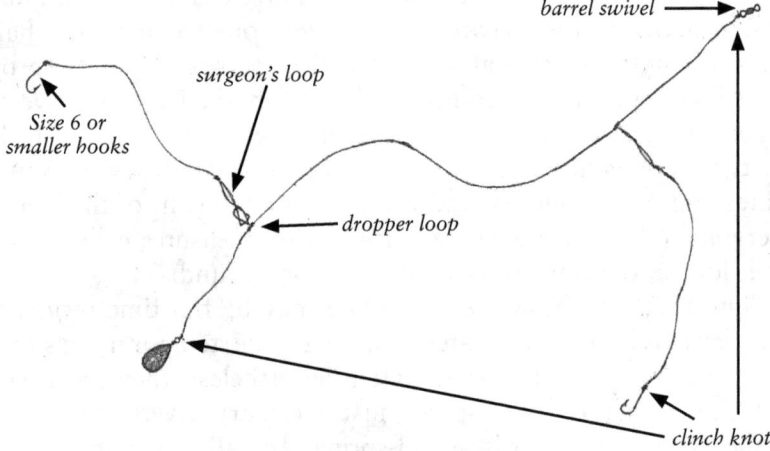

barrel swivel

surgeon's loop

Size 6 or smaller hooks

dropper loop

clinch knot

Figure 10a: *Basic homemade bottom rig*

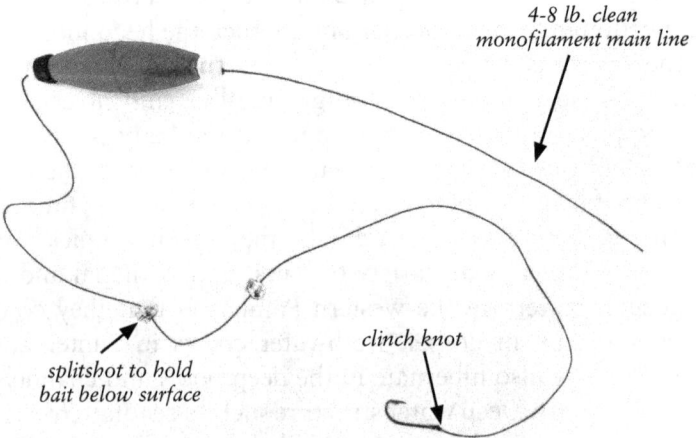

4-8 lb. clean monofilament main line

clinch knot

splitshot to hold bait below surface

Figure 10b: *Simple float rig*

Good live or cut bait includes red worms, blood worms, night crawlers, crickets, insect larvae, and small minnows. Many dedicated white perch anglers feel that grass shrimp are the ultimate bait. White perch have relatively small mouths, so natural baits should be fished on small hooks that the fish cannot easily strip and escape unhooked. In moving water small spoons and shad darts like those used in shad fishing will also draw strikes.

As the water temperatures begin to rise in spring, the perch move either downstream or upstream into the shallows to spawn. There does not seem to be any specifically favored bottom type, although a fairly flat area without structure seems to be preferred. Small protected bays located off of the main channels or outside the mouths of feeder creeks and canals feature conditions that hold schools of white perch. As with other species they tend to feed more actively in the early morning and late evening hours, but white perch frequently provide some action throughout the day.

Casting and retrieving small artificial lures along a grassy shoreline is a common technique in the mild seasons of spring and fall. Bridge abutments that extend out into narrow creeks are convenient for access by foot and can provide ideal conditions for good catches at any time of year. Spinner baits, plastic plugs, and lead head jigs weighing an eighth of an ounce or less, thrown on four to six-foot ultra-light rods with four to six-pound test line is a fun and exciting way to catch these fish. Some white perch enthusiasts feel that a red hook is an added attraction for these easily aroused fish. Others will skirt their spinner bait with a small curly tailed grub to draw more attention. Live or artificial baits elicit strikes when twitched underneath a small popping cork, and are made even more tantalizing by tipping the hook with cut bait. A faster drift or trolling speed in warm waters with either type of bait does not require an electric motor, for white perch are not frightened by the noise and turbulence of an outboard motor.

Hot temperatures of summer find white perch seeking the coolness of deep, open water in the rivers and sounds. Fishing techniques are essentially the same as previously described. By mid to late autumn the perch are again moving into the creeks, fattening themselves in preparation to hunker down for winter.

White perch are truly every man's fish. They do not require expensive equipment and are easily accessible from shore or in a small boat. Compared to the more glamorous fish in the Pamlico watershed, they fight very hard for their diminutive size, and are willing and able to take a large assortment of bait. White perch are an excellent choice of quarry for introducing beginners of any age to the sport of fishing. And on top of all that, the experience is relived in fine flavor at supper time.

*"Ripple in still water, When there is no pebble tossed,
Nor wind to blow.
Reach out your hand if your cup be empty, If your cup is full
may it be again. Let it be known there is a fountain, That was
not made by the hands of men."*
—from *Ripple*, The Grateful Dead

Chapter 7
Tarpon

Megalops atlanticus

❖ ❖ ❖

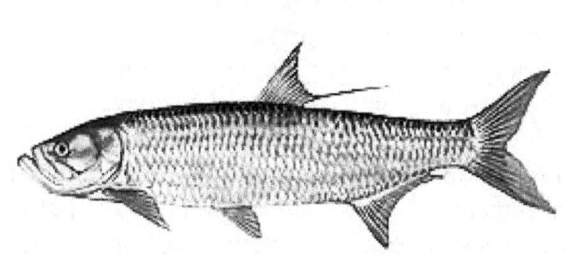

Special thanks to Captain Mitchell Blake/Fish IBX for consultation.

The old, big drum that spawn in the waters of the western Pamlico in mid to late summer have traditionally set the sport fishing bar for most recreational fishermen in the region. But for some there is a higher calling against which to measure one's patience, stamina, and skill. Just as uncompromising anglers in western NC hold up the muskellunge as the ultimate challenge in sport fishing, their compatriots in the east consider tarpon fishing an elite passion. For inner banks fishermen the tarpon is the holy grail of game fish.

Rod and reel fishing for tarpon in the Pamlico and its tributaries is said to have been first developed between the mid-sixties and late seventies. Depending on one's source of information, the identity of the individuals who initiated the fishery and the exact locale tends to vary somewhat. There is a lot that remains unknown about tarpon, including the significance of their sojourn to Tar Heel waters, which only serves to further elevate the stature of these striking creatures.

Tarpon are known to be a prehistoric species, dating back about 125 million years, and resemble a large herring. They are primarily denizens of the warm Atlantic seas, from the central coast of Brazil to the west coast of Africa, and throughout the Gulf of Mexico and Caribbean. Adult Tarpon have the ability to travel long distances, documented up to 1,200 miles. The northern limit of their summer migration along the east coast of the United States is normally the Virginia barrier islands and lower Chesapeake Bay.

Life for tarpon begins in the spring and summer over 100 miles off shore, where mature adults gather to release their sperm and eggs into the open ocean for fertilization, and is thought to be associated with the full and new moons. The eggs hatch as larvae looking like tiny, transparent eels. With limited capacity for swimming, they travel a gauntlet of various habitats over the next month, until reaching their estuarine nursery grounds in the shallow back bays and creeks as three to four-inch juveniles looking like miniature adults. These stagnant areas offer protection from some predators who cannot tolerate low oxygen environments. As they are in adulthood, baby tarpon are equipped with a swim bladder containing spongy tissue that allows them to obtain oxygen by rolling on the surface to gulp air, in addition to taking in oxygen from the water through their gills. During this period their diet consists mainly of small crustaceans and worms, and is expanded to include shrimp, crabs, and fish as they grow.

The presence of larvae off the U.S. coast as far north as North Carolina indicates that spawning probably occurs to some extent along the entire east coast range. Occasional reports of juvenile and sub-adult tarpon turning up in gill nets, being caught on hook and line, and being found cold stunned reveals that the Pamlico does indeed support young fish from time to time. However, its suitability to sustain a viable nursery population is highly questionable.

Tarpon grow slowly and do not achieve sexual maturity until approximately eight to ten years of age, with males maturing before females. Males are sexually mature at just shy of four feet and females at about four and a half feet. As sub-adults grow they continue to move to larger bodies of water until they join schools of mature adults in the ocean. The average adult fish is about six feet in length, weighs 150 pounds, and is fifteen to thirty years old. Females have been documented at over eight feet and up to 280 pounds. Longevity of life may exceed eighty years. Their slow rate of growth and maturity renders tarpon especially vulnerable to overfishing and loss of habitat, and thus, declines in populations are difficult to rebuild. As in most parts of the world, tarpon are not considered to have much food value and are a catch and release fishery on the inner banks.

Fortunately for inner banks tarpon fishermen, it is large adults that visit the region each summer. The season may begin in June and end in early September, depending on temperature and salinity, with tarpon appearing earlier and further in-land in a dry year, reportedly as far upstream as Washington. Pamlico tarpon prefer to stay in areas with about ten to twenty feet of water, usually in the open sound and river mouths. The general belief is that the tarpon bite is better with at least some ripple on the water, although much easier to spot on a dead calm day. A warm, light to moderate breeze out of the south or west is ideal, and if a north wind should drop the water temperature even a few degrees the fish may quit feeding for days. The best bite is thought to take place within three to five days of a full moon in July and August, often coinciding with the moon rise, or early in the morning during the new moon. Tarpon are nocturnally active feeders, but fishermen must be aware of tackle requirements when fishing natural baits at night, which are designed to reduce deep hooking of old red drum that often frequent the same areas.

Because of the water depth and relative lack of clarity, inner banks tarpon can be difficult to sight. Still, die hard tarpon anglers will spend hours scouting to locate a school, which are often seen rolling at the surface on calm days. Even in a light chop, their silver mirror-like scales reflect the rays of the sun. Adult tarpon do not always gulp air when rolling and are not obligated to do so under well oxygenated conditions. Rather, it is believed to be a learned habit, and is not necessarily associated with feeding. When not actually seen rolling, it is possible to hear tarpon expelling used air from their swim bladders, and then gulping a mouthful of fresh air. A trail of small bubbles rising to the surface might indicate the presence of tarpon below, releasing spurts of air as they swim. Schools of tarpon may move in a purposeful direction as they roll, or move about in a more playful, less focused manner. They are not commonly seen crashing bait fish at the surface, but now and then an individual will jump free of the water for reasons uncertain.

One of the ideal scenarios for finding tarpon in the inner banks rivers is in locating an interface between low oxygen freshwater, moving downstream, where it meets saltier water from the sound containing more available oxygen. It is sometimes recognizable by a change in color, from a more tannic and turbid hue to a clearer green/ aqua, and is more defined in the days following a significant regional rain. It is thought that the poorly oxygenated water forces a high concentration of crabs and other bait species to move ahead of it in search of more oxygen. Such areas can also be recognized by crabs swimming on the surface. The tarpon are often there for the feast.

While scouting for tarpon or when the fishing is slow, anglers can troll top water or subsurface plugs and should keep a rod rigged with a lure to cast toward sighted fish. Strikes at lures are uncommon on the Pamlico, but it does happen on rare occasions. Trolling can produce the added benefit of picking up a fresh bait specimen such as bluefish or Spanish mackerel. Tarpon spook easily, so places known to hold tarpon should be approached quietly. Schools should be given a conservative distance when attempting to anchor ahead of the fish in their anticipated direction of movement. The standard accepted distance for fishing from other boats is 200 yards in order to avoid tangling with other boats, anchors, and lines. Even with the best precautions anglers may need to release the anchor line and move quickly to maneuver a fish away from or out of entanglement with other anglers, channel markers, or other structure. A small buoy attached to the anchor line serves as a marker for relocating the anchor.

The primary technique for inner banks tarpon fishing involves enticing the fish to take whole dead or live baits on bottom rigs, or suspended at various depths in the water column beneath a float while at anchor. Rods, reels, and rigging are similar to that used for big drum except that the tackle should be heavy enough to handle a fish twice the size and strength of a mature old drum, and far more athletic. In order to avoid overstressing the fish, the goal should be to fight the fish with maximum pressure, bringing it to the boat in fifteen minutes or less. Tarpon can be caught on lighter tackle, but prolonged fight time will increase the chance of exhausting the fish and make it more susceptible to mortality following release. To draw fish close to the boat, chumming techniques identical to that used for old drum are deployed.

Rods in the heavy action class from six and a half to seven and a half feet should be equipped with extra-large spinning reels or conventional reels capable of holding at least 250 yards of line rated thirty to fifty-pounds test in strength. Recommended drag set is twenty to twenty-five percent of the main line strength, with the rod tip held at a forty-five to ninety-degree angle in relationship to the line. For example, a reel spooled with thirty pound test is set for five to eight pounds. A handheld fish scale is an accurate way to check drag pressure. Alternatively, some anglers prefer a tighter drag set, making a hook set unnecessary.

There are two schools of thought that apply to terminal rigging. Some experts prefer a progression of strength between the mainline and the hook (see fig. 11). For them, a leader long enough to be wound onto the reel four to five times as the fish nears the boat is of key importance. It allows more control when the fish is close up, prevents break off due to chafing against the body of the fish or boat, and provides the ability to safely grab the leader by hand while disengaging the hook. It will also render the many sting rays that will be caught during a tarpon outing easier to subdue and release. The wind-on leader should consist of 80-125 pound test monofilament or fluorocarbon line, typically ten to twelve feet in length, depending on the length of the rod. To connect the main running line to the wind-on leader, the main line is tied into a Bimini Twist about two feet long to form a loop, but a Surgeons Loop or Spider Hitch will also suffice, particularly when joining a main line and wind-on leader of the same material. A Uni-knot, Blood knot, or Yucatan can then be used to tie the mainline loop to the proximal end of the wind-on leader. A two to three-ounce egg sinker with a bead on each end is then threaded onto the leader, and may or may not be fixed in place with crimps. At the distal end of the leader, a 150 pound barrel swivel is tied on with a Clinch knot, Palomar knot, or Uni-knot. Finally, a three to four-foot length of 120-150 pound monofilament shock line is tied onto the other end of the barrel swivel and to an 8/0-12/0 J-hook, 8/0-16/0 circle or octopus hook, or snelled hook using Clinch knot, Uni-knot, or Palomar knot. All knots (see Appendix B) should be trimmed neatly to reduce friction on the rod guides when casting and prevent tangling with line on the spool.

Alternatively, the rigging is designed to minimize connections, use crimps in place of some knots, and thereby reduce chances of tackle failure (see fig. 12). For example, various knots as outlined above are used to tie a single strand of main line to a 100-150 pound snap swivel, which is in turn snapped through a crimped loop on the proximal end of the leader. The leader is then threaded through an egg sinker, which is crimped in place twelve to eighteen inches above a hook that is secured on another crimped loop. A separate shock line is eliminated altogether. The length of leader and sinker beneath the swivel can then be adjusted to allow setting the bait at the desired depth. Some anglers choose a shorter leader, only the length of the rod, which is not wound in past the rod tip, or will double the main line back to the reel if using braided line. They rightly point out that the lighter, thinner main line is more aerodynamic, and without knots will reduce friction on the reel and rod guides, thus increasing cast distance. In the case of a single strand of main line, the absence of a knot within the line on the reel will have the added benefit of reducing the chance for tangles on the reel. Regardless, enough length of leader is still available for safe hook removal.

Simpler still (see fig. 13), a fifty-pound braided main line is connected directly to a six to seven-foot length of 80-120 pound monofilament or fluorocarbon leader, using a barrel swivel or Yucatan knot. The hook is tied on or crimped onto the end of the leader, and a sinker slider (aka "fish finder") is lightly crimped twenty-four to thirty inches above the hook. A one to four-ounce diamond sinker can then be secured for bottom fishing, or a balloon can be attached as a float rig.

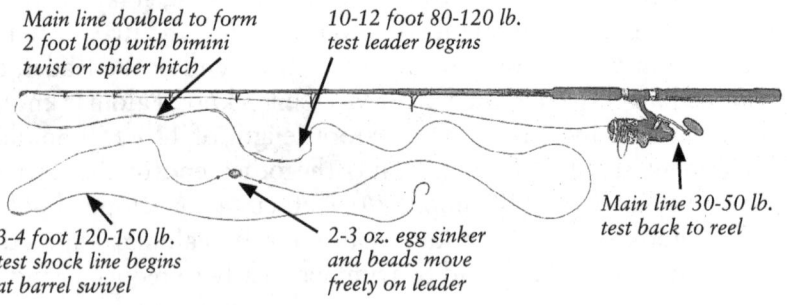

Main line doubled to form 2 foot loop with bimini twist or spider hitch

10-12 foot 80-120 lb. test leader begins

3-4 foot 120-150 lb. test shock line begins at barrel swivel

2-3 oz. egg sinker and beads move freely on leader

Main line 30-50 lb. test back to reel

Figure 11

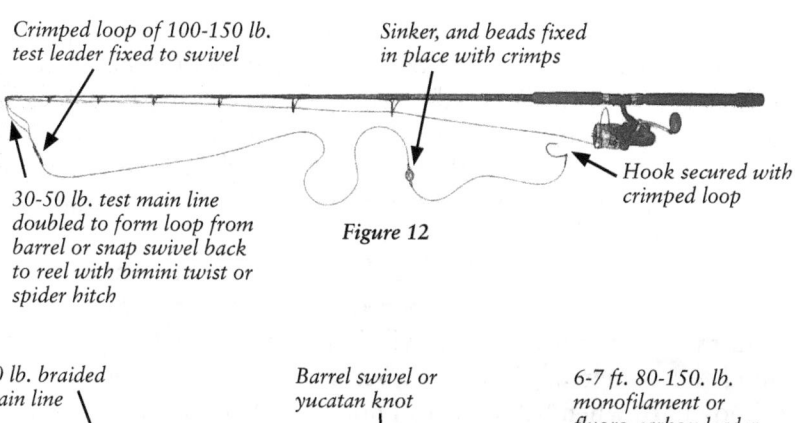

Crimped loop of 100-150 lb. test leader fixed to swivel

Sinker, and beads fixed in place with crimps

30-50 lb. test main line doubled to form loop from barrel or snap swivel back to reel with bimini twist or spider hitch

Hook secured with crimped loop

Figure 12

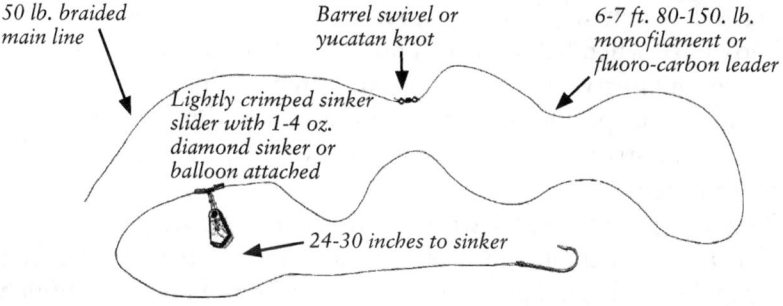

50 lb. braided main line

Barrel swivel or yucatan knot

6-7 ft. 80-150. lb. monofilament or fluoro-carbon leader

Lightly crimped sinker slider with 1-4 oz. diamond sinker or balloon attached

24-30 inches to sinker

Figure 13

The latter set ups (see figs. 12 and 13) are conducive for fishing either live or dead bait under a float, whereas the float can be conveniently attached to the swivel at the connection between the main line and leader (see fig. 12), or in place of the sinker along the leader (see fig. 13). Balloons are an effective, inexpensive float device that will easily break off when the action begins following a tarpon strike. Several rods are typically set out in order to methodically cover the entire water column. Alternatively, some fishermen let the bait move up and down freely, without sinker or float, corresponding with the forces of wind, waves, and current.

Tarpon will hit a number of cut or whole dead baits. Some of the favorites include fresh croaker, menhaden, spot, and mullet. The emphasis is on freshness, preferably caught and put on ice the same day. Bait fish are fished whole or cut into halves, fillets, or steaks that are four to eight inches in length and one to two inches thick. Frequent changing of baits is mandatory to maintain freshness. Most tarpon fishermen will deploy at least four to six rods at different angles around the boat. Live bait fishing for tarpon is less popular than fishing with whole dead bait or cut bait on the Pamlico, but can be effective at times. In addition to the species used for cut bait, similar sized bluefish, pinfish, and crabs are fished alive beneath floats or on the bottom with or without weights. Live bait hooks and other types should be hooked from the bait fish's top jaw and up through the nose.

Tarpon have an extremely hard, bony jaw structure, and are very difficult to hook. Most experienced anglers favor letting the fish run in the hope that the hook will lodge in the relatively soft spot behind the corner of either jaw. Some experts recommend setting the hook hard when fishing with J hooks. Either way one can expect to lose the majority of fish that strike, often during a "jump off". Predictably, a tarpon will jump with the bait within ten to twenty seconds of the strike, and average about five to six jumps during the course of a fight.

These fish are incredibly strong and usually hit with a very hard initial run. When the tarpon starts to lose momentum on the first run immediately begin applying nonstop maximum pressure. Winch the fish inward by pulling the rod back and upward, alternating with a quick down and forward motion while reeling in the slack rapidly. During each strong run point the rod tip at the fish and let it run against the drag, resuming pressure by reeling any slack in fast when the fish slows. The object is to maintain steady pressure and fight a tarpon close, letting out the minimum amount of line possible. This will reduce the chance of the line being cut by the tarpon's gill plates and hard scales, with the exception of when a tarpon jumps. Violent head shaking, flared gills, and a writhing body against a taught line sharply increase the risk of getting cut off, particularly if the fish should fall backward toward the boat and land on the line, or slice it against its hard mouth. When the tarpon jumps the angler should give the fish some slack by lowering the rod, leaning forward, and 'bowing to the silver king'. Keeping the head up can help discourage the fish from running again when tired enough to come to the boat. The leader can then be grabbed with a gloved hand, and the hook cautiously removed with a sturdy pair of pliers.

Do not attempt to take a tarpon out of the water for pictures. Due to girth and weight, their internal organs are vulnerable to damage when hoisted or dragged over the gunnels of a boat, and can easily be fatal. If the hook cannot be removed in the water, cut the leader as close as possible to the hook, which will rust and dissolve.

It has been postulated that adrenaline can make war addictive for warriors. More benignly, the sheer size, breath taking power, and spectacular shimmering leaps of western Pamlico tarpon will deliver heart pounding thrills for those fishermen with the prowess and fortitude to challenge them. May it always be so.

*"Just because you're paranoid doesn't
mean they aren't after you."*
–FROM CATCH 22, BY JOSEPH HELLER

CHAPTER 8
BLUE CRABS

Callinectes sapidus

❖ ❖ ❖

In English *Callinectes sapidus* translates to "savory beautiful swimmer." The Blue Crab's beauty may be in the eye of the beholder, but its taste is considered superior by many. Demand for its meat is evidenced by its history of being NC's top fishery based on pounds landed. Whether caught commercially or recreationally, these cranky crustaceans are valued for good reason, including hours and hours of entertainment.

Blue crabs utilize a wide variety of estuarine habitats, including intertidal marshes, sea grass beds, and soft-sediment bottoms, and are highly tolerant of various temperature and salinity ranges. They are ravenous predators and scavengers that will eat fish, clams, oysters, mussels, snails, worms, insects, and just about anything else they can ingest. Cannibalism is frequent, especially when victims are most vulnerable in the "soft-shell" stage of molting.

As a blue crab grows it must repeatedly shed its shell, or "molt", and form a new one. After shedding their old shells, they are more vulnerable to predation with a very thin, soft shell that hardens over the next two days. These soft-shell crabs are highly sought-after delicacies for crab lovers. A crab will molt up to twenty-five times during its life span, which is rarely longer than two to three years. The life cycle (see fig. 14) of the Blue Crab begins with mating between sexually mature males and females (see fig. 15). As winter ends and the waters warm, crabs emerge from hibernation in the mud of deep waters to resume eating, molting, and mating. Mating begins in early spring and continues through mid-autumn. An immature female, called a "Sally", will molt a total of about eighteen to twenty-three times before reaching maturity. The female is fertilized by the male during her last molt and only when she is soft-shelled.

When her final molt is impending, usually during her second summer, the female will release a chemical scent in her urine that will attract males. When a mature male called a "Jimmy" encounters the female, he will perform an elaborate courtship dance and release his own chemical scent in his urine to get her attention. The female responds by rocking and waving her claws, and the male continues courtship by tapping and rubbing her claws with his. Soon she will fold her claws, taking on a submissive posture, and allow the male to cradle her underneath him with his walking legs. The pair is then called a "doubler" or a "buck and rider."

Over the next two to seven days the male will carry the female until molting is imminent. During this period the male is able to protect the female from predators, and his presence assures him the female captures and stores the male's sperm in sac-like receptacles so that she can fertilize her eggs at a later time. The male stays with the female over the next forty-eight hours to protect her until her shell has re-hardened, and then releases her to migrate toward higher salinity waters, where she will spawn. During the final molting and mating process the shape (apron) on the female's abdomen changes from a "V" shape to a more rounded "U" shape. She is now called a "sook" will not molt or mate again in her life.

After migration to higher salinity waters in lower estuaries, sounds, and near-shore spawning areas, they spend winter burrowed in the mud. Spawning occurs from March through October in North Carolina, and peaks from April to August. Early reproductive females generally spawn prior to the coming winter, while those maturing later spawn the following spring. The fertilized eggs are developed internally but are forced out from under the apron, growing into a sponge like mass over about two hours and containing up to two million eggs. During the next one to two weeks the sponge changes from lemon colored to black and remains attached to her abdomen, while the larval crabs are released.

The microscopic larvae are called a "zoea" (see fig. 14) and drift on the currents out into the ocean where they go through numerous stages of development before they even look like a crab. Several stages later the zoea molt into the next larval form, termed a "megalops", which resembles a small lobster. The megalops migrates back into the sounds and rivers where it develops into a juvenile crab over about two months. It is estimated that only one of each million eggs will survive to adulthood. Causes of mortality include fungal infection, predation, suffocation in stagnant water, and exposure to extreme temperatures.

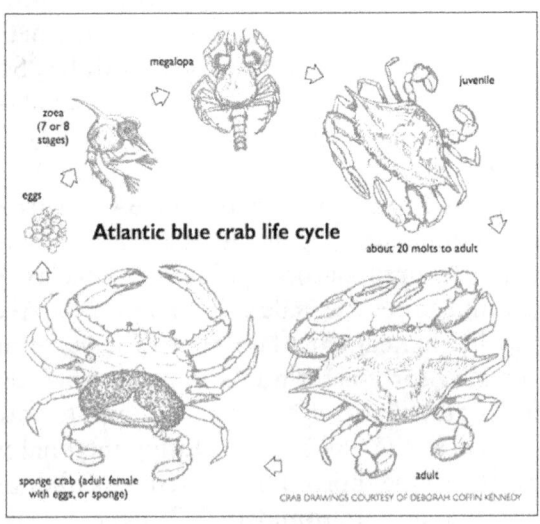

Figure 14

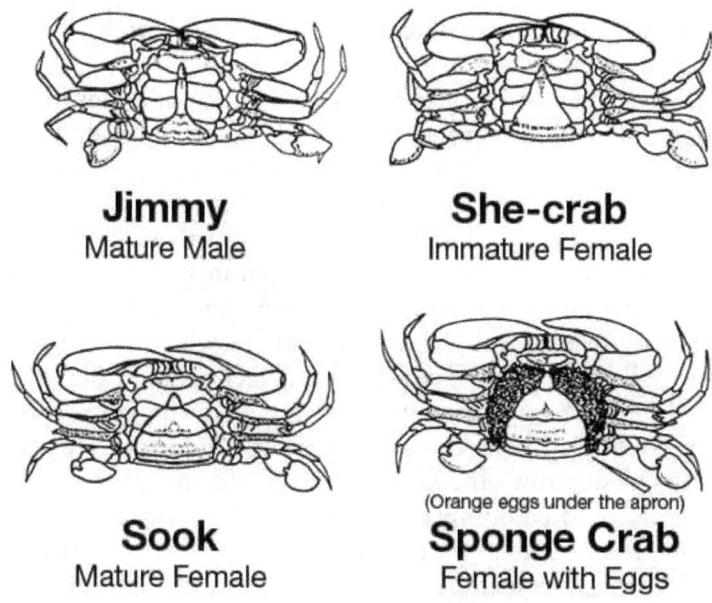

Jimmy
Mature Male

She-crab
Immature Female

Sook
Mature Female

(Orange eggs under the apron)
Sponge Crab
Female with Eggs

Figure 15: Blue crab terminology

Blue crabs experience a remarkable amount of shell exchange during a lifetime. Aside from molting, they can regenerate a leg or claw that is lost to injury. Additionally, if a crab is seized by a predator and held by a leg, it has the ability to release limbs voluntarily as an escape mechanism. The leg is regenerated during the next shedding cycle.

When treated with respect, the cantankerous blue crab can provide endless hours of outdoor fun for children and adults alike. Crabbing from a pier or bulkhead in an area crawling with crabs is low tech, inexpensive, and normally packed with action. It only requires a dip net (see fig. 16) and chicken/turkey necks or other inexpensive parts tied onto a nylon twine and weighted with a washer, nut, or small piece of scrap metal. Weights are adjusted depending on current, wind, and wave action. Lines should be lengthened according to water depth and height of the surface above the water. There are also a variety of traps that are easy to use and available for use without a license for commercial gear. Crabs can also be caught with commercial crab pots (see fig. 16) that can be used with a special recreational license purchased under regulation by the North Carolina Division of Marine Fisheries.

Excited screams and giggles are free of charge, and kids normally do not care if crabs are keepers or not. Patience and teamwork are learned naturally by crabbing with bait on a string. Just have the children take turns gently inching the crabs toward the surface, while another scoops it up with the net. The greedy feeding behavior of crabs makes them vulnerable. Even when missed or knocked off the line, they will soon be back to give the young crabbers another opportunity. An even simpler way to catch crabs is to walk along a pier or bulkhead, while looking for crabs clinging to the side of a pole, and quickly swipe them up with a net. In this case there will often be doublers. Crabs can also be spotted and scooped directly from areas of shallow, sandy bottom while wading quietly.

Keepers should be dumped from the net into a bucket or cooler with a small amount of water, and kept alive in cool shade. Like fish, crabs extract oxygen from the water using gills, but can survive for long periods out of water. As long as their gills can be kept moist, oxygen can diffuse into them.

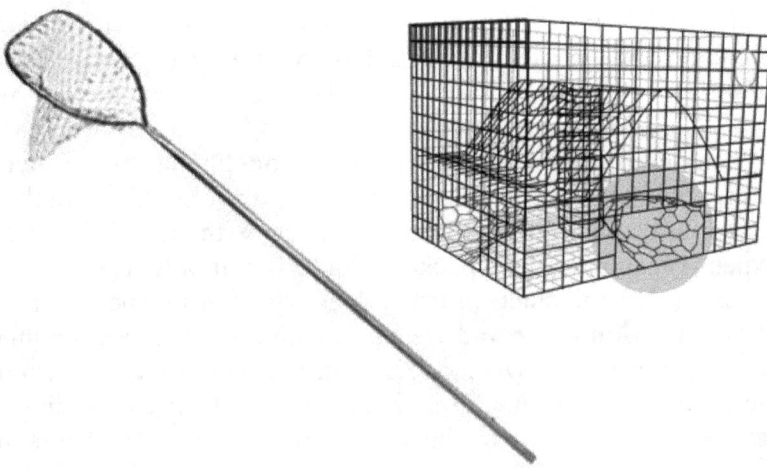

Figure 16: Typical dip net and commercial pot design

It is probably a good idea to avoid handling crabs altogether, if possible. A puncture wound or bite from a crab has potential for infection from bacteria such as *Mycobacterium marinum* and *Vibrio vulnificus*. Inevitably, a crab or two will escape onto the deck and flea for the water with astonishing speed. Prepare for this scenario by having a flip-flop or other protective object handy to suppress the crab from above, and grasp it at the base of the back fin, where the dangerous claws can do no damage.

There are those who believe that a crab can be put to sleep, simply by laying the crab on its back and rubbing its belly. However, this maneuver is not without risk. The fact is that crabs really are the grouchy, grumpy curmudgeons that they appear to be. That may be why they are called "crabs".

CHAPTER 9
SHRIMP

Rigging illustrations by Victor Cormier

❖ ❖ ❖

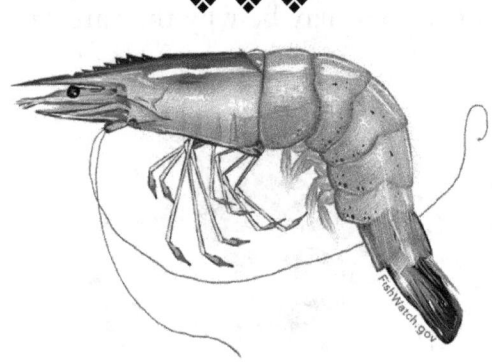

For obvious reasons shrimp is the second most economically
important fishery in North Carolina. Not only are they highly
preyed upon by humans, but they are also a very important
component of estuarine ecosystems, serving as prey for many fish
and larger crustaceans. Brown, white, and pink shrimp are the
three main species of shrimp in North Carolina. All of them are
spawned in the ocean, and are carried by tides and wind-driven
currents into estuarine nursery areas when they are young, where it
is relatively safe and there is plenty of food. They are omnivorous
and eat organic matter produced by the decomposition of other
plant and animal organisms, as well as small invertebrates and fish.
During this period, they double in size about every two weeks, prior
to swimming out into the ocean when almost full grown. Shrimp
live a maximum of eighteen to twenty-four months. Salinity and
temperature are the primary controlling factors in their survival,

distribution, and growth. Following a cold winter, the shrimp population will be small in the spring. During a rainy year with low salinities in the sounds, the shrimp will move out into the ocean before fully grown.

Pink shrimp account for only about five percent of landings in North Carolina. They live to about twenty-four months and grow the longest, up to eleven inches. Otherwise, they are similar to brown and white shrimp in patterns of behavior and development, and will not be discussed here in further detail.

Bulk heading, ditching, and disposal of dredged material, and runoff from agriculture, silviculture, and municipal or residential development can reduce the suitability and value of some estuarine habitats as nursery areas. Bulk heading reduces the marsh-water interface that is a critical habitat for post-larval and juvenile shrimp. Excessive ditching and canals not only contribute to excessive surface drainage, which can affect salinity patterns in estuaries and the influx of shrimp, but can contribute substantial amounts of pesticides, herbicides and sediments to the ecosystem.

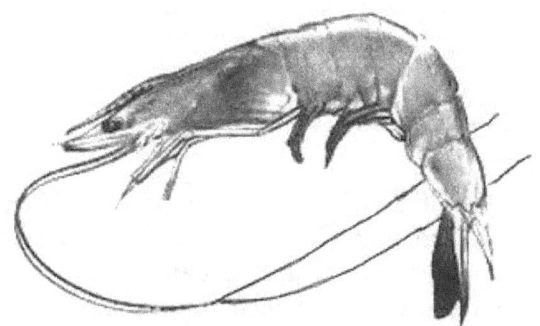

Figure 17: Brown Shrimp (Farfantepenaeus aztecus)

Brown Shrimp (see fig. 17) occur from Massachusetts to the Florida Keys, and all along the Gulf of Mexico to the Yucatan Peninsula. They are the most abundant shrimp species along the NC coast and account for about sixty-seven percent of the state's commercial shrimp landings. In late winter and early spring brown shrimp are spawned in the ocean and the larvae are transported by the tides and wind-driven currents into the estuaries. In North Carolina they spend March through June in nursery areas, migrating to larger bays and eventually the open sounds toward the nearest inlet as they grow. Growth rates and movement may vary considerably due to differences in water temperature, salinity, and food availability. They prefer loose peat and sandy mud bottoms, but may frequent sand, silt, or clay mixed with rock and shell fragments. Brown shrimp sometimes burrow in response to low temperatures, which may serve as a mechanism for moderating temperature, as well as avoiding predation. Most brown shrimp are caught in the summer and have a life span of about eighteen months, and grow as large as nine inches.

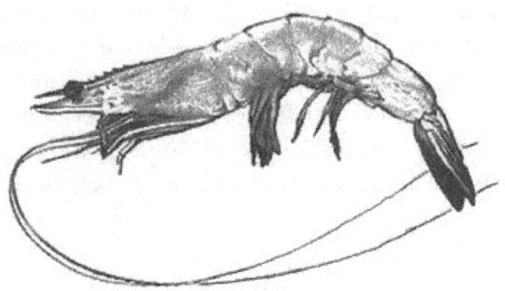

Figure 18: White shrimp (Litopanaeus setiferus)

White shrimp (see fig. 18), sometimes called "green tails", co-exist with brown and pink shrimp along the Atlantic and gulf coasts. They are the second most abundant species in NC and account for about twenty-eight percent of the harvest. Spawned in the ocean from March through November, white shrimp enter the estuaries from June until September, borne by tides and wind-driven currents. Few white shrimp live as long as one year, but they have a potential life-span of up to twenty-four months, and can grow to eight inches. They are harvested primarily in the fall after, beginning their migration to the inlets. Like brown shrimp, white shrimp prefer muddy bottoms, with loose peat and sandy mud for temperature stability, protection, and food availability.

Cast-netting (see Chapter 11) is the most common method for catching shrimp among recreational fishermen. Commercially available shrimp traps and seine netting (see Chapter 11) are also inexpensive, low tech methods for capturing them. Because of the lack of tidal currents in much of the region, shrimp traps that are dependent on bait may be more effective. Cans of cat food with holes poked in them placed in the bait chamber are a typical example of bait for shrimp pots. A license can be purchased for shrimp "pound" traps for use in areas featuring tidal currents. As of this publication, a recreational license is also available for trawling a commercial fishing style net behind a power boat, but the practice remains controversial due to bottom disturbance and finfish by-catch. Be sure to check regulations with the North Carolina Division of Marine Fisheries for use of any type gear.

An easy way to find shrimp is to make a small wake with a boat and watch as the wake hits the marsh. If there are shrimp hanging along the edge of the marsh, they will begin "popping" out of the water. Cast-netting near lighted docks at night can be very effective. In more recent years, some NC fisherman have begun adopting a technique known as "shrimp-baiting," where fish meal combined with a binder to form a "bait ball" is dropped into an area to attract shrimp for easier cast-netting. The most common bait is a mixture of powdered clay and fish meal made from ground menhaden. Flour, corn meal, cat food, and chicken feed can also be used in bait balls. Mud or Portland cement can also serve as the binding agent, and there are other products available that make the process quick and easy. The bait balls should range in size from a tennis ball to a softball and then flattened out similar to a hamburger. Long poles are planted in the bottom to mark a specific location, and then bait is placed in the water near the pole. After waiting several minutes the cast net is thrown in close proximity to the bait, where the shrimp should be more concentrated.

The shrimp will need to be kept alive in some type of aerated live well system or perhaps overboard in a minnow bucket. A standard five gallon bucket fitted with an electric aerator will usually suffice, but more elaborate systems are available on the market, or built into many boats.

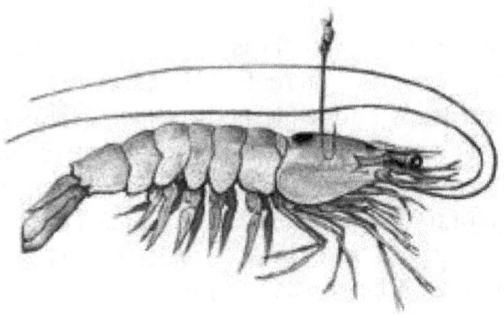

Figure 19

Shrimp are probably the best all-around live bait for the salt and brackish water species found along the Inner Banks. They can be fished as cut bait or whole when dead, but suspending a live shrimp below a popping cork or other float rig is the most common and effective way of baiting with shrimp. To take maximum advantage of their natural kicking action, run the hook crosswise through the hard ridge at the top of the head (see fig. 19), taking care to avoid the dark spot inside the head, where vital organs are located. This style of hooking is ideal for random drifting or passively drifting with current. The disadvantage is that the hookup is flimsy, and the shrimp will likely pull off when actively popping the cork and is more easily stolen of the hook by smaller fish.

Figure 20

Alternatively, run the hook point under the chin (see fig. 20), so that it exits through the hard ridge at the top/center of the head, again taking care to avoid the dark spot. In this way the hookup will be more stable, allow greater casting distance, and make it easier to retrieve without losing the bait.

Figure 21

Another method used when casting distance and aggressively popping the cork is critical, is to thread the shrimp through its tail (see fig. 21) to reduce the chances of the shrimp tearing off even further. After breaking off the tail fan, thread the hook through the center of the tail until the entire shank is hidden and push the point through the underside of the tail. Removal of the shrimp's tail fan will emit a scent that attracts fish. A live bait style hook will help prevent the shrimp from sliding off the hook.

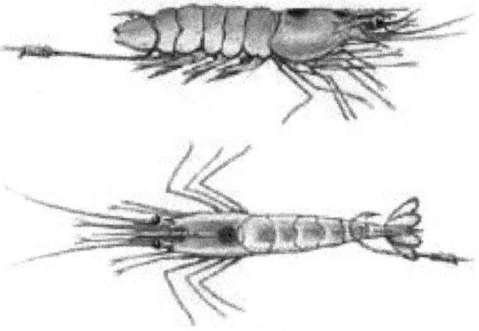

Figure 22

A final way to rig a shrimp for basic casting and drift-fishing is to run the hook through the tip of the tail (see fig. 22), either crosswise or up through the center of the tail. Many fishermen prefer this method because it keeps the hook clear of bottom snags, allows the shrimp to kick freely, and provides some measure of hookup stability. The tail fan can be left on, or removed to provide additional scent.

The added bonus of fishing with live shrimp is that they are by far the best bait for human consumption. At the end of the day, the left-over bait will make a tasty appetizer prior to eating fresh fish.

"The man had a sure palate cover'd o'er
With brass or steel, that on the rocky shore
First broke the oozy oyster's pearly coat
And risqu'd the living morsel down his throat."
　　　　　　　　　　　　　　　　–JOHN GAY, 1685-1732

CHAPTER 10
EASTERN OYSTER

Crassostrea virginica

❖ ❖ ❖

Contemplate the lowly oyster. In appearance it might be seen as a homely, perhaps downright ugly creature. After being plucked from a shell covered with fishy mud and grit, the highly prized pearls that it generates hang elegantly on the necklines of the rich and famous. Served as Oysters Rockefeller in the upscale restaurants of New York and other cosmopolitan centers, or dumped on a backyard picnic table in steaming piles, the oyster remains a favorite on the palate. Its shells are ground up for marketing as human calcium supplements and many an oyster shell has met its final destiny as pavement for someone's driveway. For generations it has been thought to enhance libido, and ironically should always be approached with caution for disease.

The eastern oyster is a naturally occurring inhabitant of the western Atlantic, stretching from the Gulf of St. Lawrence on the Canadian coast to the Gulf of Mexico and Caribbean Sea. It can tolerate a broad range of salinity, temperature, turbidity, and oxygen levels, all of which make it readily adaptable to the constantly changing conditions in an estuary. In areas of lunar tidal movement, closer to NC's inlets, many oysters are "intertidal", growing between the average high and low tide levels, and are fully exposed during periods of low tide. In the Western Pamlico most oysters are "subtidal" and remain submerged for the most part due to the lack of lunar tidal influence.

Oysters are bivalve mollusks that can live up to forty years and grow up to eight inches. They are typically separate male and females in sex, but are capable of changing sex about once each year. Natural populations maintain an essentially balanced sex ratio. However, conditions of stress, such as pollution or food shortage, may result in a higher proportion of males. Sexual organs may develop in oysters at two to three months of age, and fully developed oysters entering their first summer may spawn. Their fastest rate of growth is the highest during the first six months, after the spat sets (see fig. 23), and declines thereafter. Seasonally, oysters grow faster during the spring and fall in North Carolina, and reach market size at three inches in eighteen to twenty-four months. During the warmer months of spawning season, oysters grow their gonads for production of eggs and sperm, and are not as tasty because they are packed with gonads or are too watery after spawning. Accordingly, oysters are harvested from October to March with tongs, rakes, or by hand, in intertidal areas and shallow water along coastal North Carolina. They are also caught by dredges in parts of the Pamlico Sound, although the sustainability of this practice is debatable.

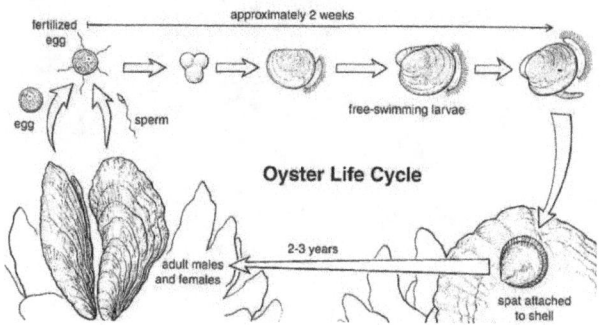

Figure 23: Oyster life cycle

Oysters have a natural tendency to build their own habitat, a strategy that has several survival benefits. As the larval stage ends during the warmest months, larvae must find a suitable place to attach or they will perish. They respond to a protein on the surface of living or dead adult oyster shells, which are their preferred surface for settlement and growth. Thus, the shells of the oyster are its own habitat substrate and should be re-deployed or "re-cycled" back into the water.

Oysters and oyster reefs provide an excellent habitat for a variety of fish and crustaceans, and perform an important role in maintaining water quality, when present in sufficient numbers. Restored and natural oyster reefs in the Neuse river and Pamlico sound have been shown to attract large numbers of clams, amphipods, worms, and grass shrimp. In turn, the reef community provides abundant foraging for commercially and recreationally important species including red and black drum, spot, gray trout, speckled trout, flounder, croaker, sheep head, Spanish mackerel, and blue crabs. Each mature oyster filters about forty-five gallons of water per day (see fig. 24). The loss of filtering capacity provided by a fully functional oyster population removes a natural means for recycling nutrients and organic material, controlling harmful algae blooms and bacterial contamination, and reducing turbidity. Oyster reefs or "rocks" can also stabilize shoreline erosion by modifying wave action and currents in areas where they are abundant.

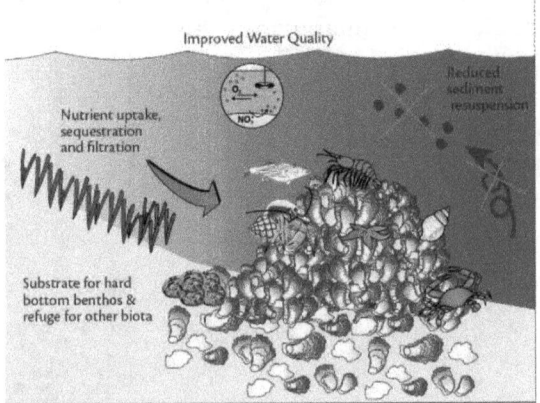

Figure 24: Ecosystem benefits provided by oysters

Despite its impressive record of goods and services, the oyster has been historically taken for granted, and their existence in our estuary today is only a small fraction of what it once was. Poor water quality, disease, over-harvesting, and habitat destruction have all contributed to the dramatic decline in North Carolina's estuarine oyster stocks. In 1889, Lieutenant Francis Winslow of the U.S. Navy published a survey of North Carolina's sounds, with respect to oysters and potential oyster habitat. Public areas, vulnerable to hand harvest methods, were felt to be in degraded condition, even at that time. Still he was able to identify over 8,000 acres of natural oyster beds, much of which was located in the middle and western portions of the Pamlico. Commercial harvests in North Carolina of over a million bushels per year occurred in that era, and remained the most valuable shellfish fishery until the 1970s. The harvest sank to an all-time low of 38,455 bushels in the year 2000. Since then, the yearly harvest has gradually climbed back to over 180,000 bushels in the year of 2010, which represented combined mechanical and hand harvesting methods. It has since gradually declined again as of this publication. And yet all is not lost. The volume of harvest coming from private bottom leased from the state has increased, possibly reflecting a budding oyster farming industry. North Carolina and other mid-Atlantic states may be turning the corner in the quest to replenish this cornerstone species. The battle is centered on development of oysters that can conquer the effects of disease by employing a two-pronged strategy of interdependent factors; rapid growth and disease resistance.

Dermo disease (*Perkinsis marinarus*) thrives in warm waters of high salinity. Oysters can live and grow robustly in salinities slightly lower than those tolerated by Dermo, which does not cause serious mortality below salinities of 12 to 15 ppt. From the Pamlico Sound southward, Dermo attacks, emaciates, and kills oysters after the second summer when the water is hottest and saltiest, before growing to marketable size in their third year.

MSX disease (*Haplosporidium nelsoni*) is an oyster pathogen that has been lethal to the oyster population in the Chesapeake Bay, and is present in North Carolina waters, although to a much less degree. However, MSX can kill oysters at any age, young or old. Apart from disease, oyster survival is dependent on water quality with sufficient oxygen, stable salinity patterns, suitable attachment surfaces, adequate food supplies, and sufficient water flow.

As of this publication, North Carolina has instituted two promising programs that are designed to take advantage of optimal growing conditions in the race to allow healthier oysters to reach marketable size before being stricken with disease. NC Sea Grant and NC Division of Marine Fisheries (DMF) have partnered to create the now popular NC Under Dock Oyster Culture Program, which permits the opportunity for people to grow oysters in suspended cages under their coastal docks or piers in waters approved for the harvest of shellfish. DMF has also undertaken the building of large oyster sanctuaries in the Pamlico on select sites that have historically supported large natural reefs. They are constructed in part from massive quantities of recycled oyster shells collected from businesses and private individuals. These sanctuaries are designed for reef growth high in the water column and are off limits to harvesting. As an oyster reef expands upward in the water column, oysters further from the bottom are less susceptible to the smothering effect of sedimentation and deadly periods of depleted oxygen. An oyster that expends less energy pumping water to breathe and filter sediment can devote more energy to growth, development, and immunity. By allowing oysters to grow in ideal conditions and free from harvest pressure, it is hoped that a strain of oysters resistant to disease will eventually dominate the sanctuaries through the process of natural selection, thus generating a continual stock of oysters with immunity to Dermo and MSX that will ultimately re-populate the sounds.

Perhaps with continued conservative management of the fishery, ingenuity for growth and survival, and restoration of water quality the long-term outlook for oysters will improve.

Alice "Nana" Boettger at Cape Hatteras, circa 1960

"We truly have an ancient part of the brain that was about survival when we were prey but we seem to have gone past prey. We eat everything and nothing eats us."
–Nick Nolte

Chapter 11
Bait Species
❖ ❖ ❖

All of the species discussed here can be used as cut or live bait. They are usually caught with the simple equipment shown in fig. 25, either from a dock, shoreline, or from a boat, but may require some stalking and stealth before they can be captured.

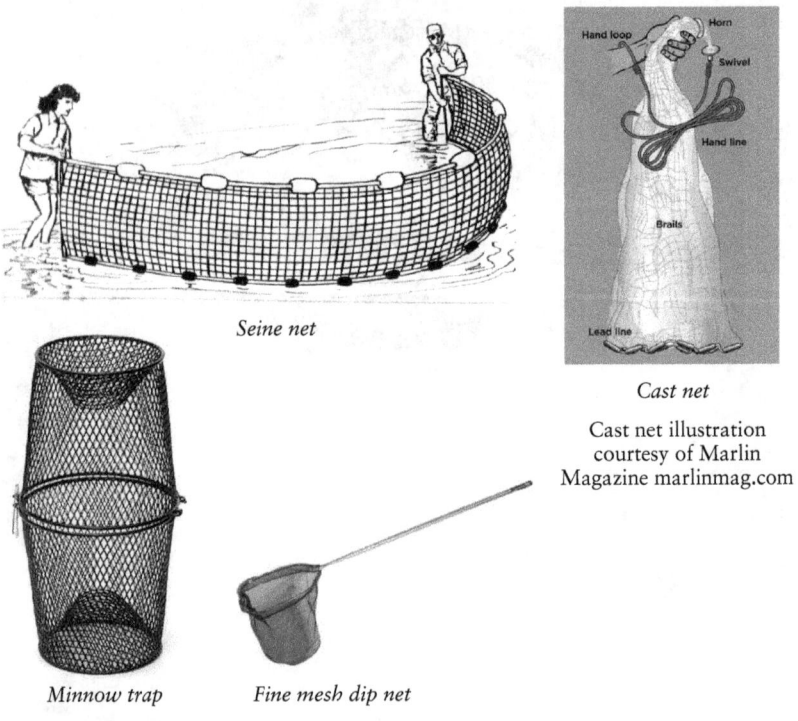

Seine net

Cast net

Cast net illustration
courtesy of Marlin
Magazine marlinmag.com

Minnow trap   *Fine mesh dip net*

Figure 25: *Bait fishing equipment*

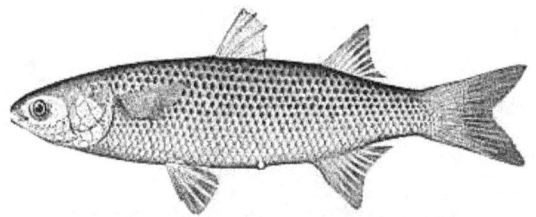

Figure 26: Striped mullet (Mugil cephalus)

Striped mullet are probably the most popularly used form of cut bait among fishermen in the western Pamlico, and are very plentiful in North Carolina estuarine waters. The flesh is firm and stays on the hook well. The coloring is bluish-gray or green above, shading to silver on the sides with distinct horizontal black stripes, and white below (see fig. 26). When under six inches long they do not have stripes. They usually inhabit inshore marine waters, estuaries, and rivers. Adults move off shore in late fall and winter to spawn, the young moving inshore and up rivers in spring when at about one inch in length. Sometimes referred to as "popeye" mullet or often as "jumpin'" mullet for its multiple high leaps from the water, striped mullet are adaptive to extremely different environments. They occur worldwide in tropic, sub tropic, and warm temperate waters from Nova Scotia to Brazil on the Atlantic coast. Striped mullet tolerate salinity from 0 to 81 ppt (hypersaline), and temperatures from forty-one to ninety-eight point six degrees Fahrenheit. Growth is up to three feet in length, but usually less than twenty inches. They feed on plankton and invertebrates, and gulp and filter sediment for particulate organic matter.

Striped mullet are a significant source of commercial and subsistence fishing in many parts of the world. Although the flesh is very oily, they can be excellent when grilled or smoked fresh from the water. The roe is considered quite good fried by some locals along the Pamlico.

Figure 27: White mullet (Mugil curema)

White mullet are plentiful in coastal waters from Massachusetts to Brazil, sometimes entering fresh water. Juveniles of the species are commonly found along with striped mullet during the summer months in North Carolina estuarine habitats. In North Carolina they return to the sea in early fall, presumably migrating southward to Florida or beyond. Instead of spawning in the fall, white mullet spawn at sea in the spring, near the edge of the continental shelf in their southerly range. However, spawning activity has not been documented in North Carolina waters, and white mullet older than age one are really seen north of Florida. Very similar to striped mullet in appearance, the white mullet lacks side bars when less than about six inches in length (see fig. 27). However, there are nine soft fin rays in the anal fin, instead of eight as in the striped mullet, and a dark blotch present at the base of the pectoral fin. Food sources and feeding habits are essentially identical to striped mullet. They are typically less than one pound, but reportedly can reach up to three pounds. Also known for its jumping ability, it is an excellent choice of cut bait, or live bait when younger.

The term "finger mullet" usually refers to young mullets under about six inches, either striped or white mullet, by far the two most common species found in the Pamlico. At that stage of development, they can be difficult to tell apart, but both species are excellent bait fish. Speckled trout, small to medium red drum, and southern flounder will readily take finger mullets fished as live bait. Mullets are a schooling fish and easily caught with a cast net when spotted from a boat or shore. They are also commonly seen jumping from the water.

Why do mullets jump? There are three prevailing theories: evasion of predators, a mechanism for respiration, and ridding themselves of parasites. Typically, several fish in a school will jump simultaneously to avoid predators, retaining an upright posture and re-entering the water cleanly. As a respiratory mechanism a single fish does a slower, shorter leap, sometimes flipping onto its side or back, or rolling at the surface. They can also be seen swimming at the surface with their head above water. Some research suggests that mullet use these techniques as a way to trap air in a pocket near the back of their throat, allowing them to use it as a supplement for activity in water of low oxygen concentration.

Figure 28: Atlantic menhaden (Brevoortia tyrannus)

Atlantic menhaden, also known as "bunker", "fatback", and "pogey", occupy special ecologic, socioeconomic, and cultural niches along their range from Nova Scotia to Florida. Vast schools of menhaden were once common along the entire Atlantic coast of the United States, with schools often spanning more than a mile in diameter. Menhaden populations have declined steadily since the early 1980s, but compact schools of hundreds or thousands may still be seen rippling on the surface throughout the Pamlico, often feeding with their snouts and backs above the water.

Adult menhaden average twelve to fifteen inches in length. Coloration is dark blue-green on top, silvery sides, with fins and belly having a yellow brassy luster. A large dark spot is located behind the gill cover, followed by several smaller spots (see fig. 28). They spawn in the open ocean throughout the year where eggs hatch at sea and are transported to estuaries by ocean currents over one to three months. Menhaden tolerate a wide range of salinity, but are generally associated with higher salinity environments as they grow into adulthood. Thus, intermittent absence of mature adults in the western Pamlico may be an indicator of freshwater input.

Primarily filter feeders on plankton and decaying plant matter, menhaden are thought to be second only to oysters in their capacity to help maintain overall estuarine health. As oysters became decimated along parts of the Atlantic coast during the twentieth century, menhaden have become even more important as filters. By ingesting algae and other phytoplankton, menhaden are capable of removing a significant percentage of the excess nitrogen and phosphorus that cause algal overgrowth (see Chapter 1).

Menhaden are also the principle source of forage for many popular sport and commercial fish, which rely on juvenile menhaden for the bulk of their diet. Accordingly, they are highly valued as live or cut bait by rod and reel fishermen. Menhaden are an oily fish packed with tiny bones, and are not considered desirable to eat by most humans. Yet the catch along the Atlantic coast has regularly exceeded the tonnage of all other species combined. They are cooked and reduced to fish meal and oil. The meal is dried, ground up, and incorporated as a high-protein feed component for livestock and pets. The oil can also be used to make omega-3 fatty oil, a dietary supplement said to fight heart disease.

Purse seining was the traditional method of harvesting menhaden, where a pair of long boats were deployed in which as many as forty men hauled and closed a net around a school of fish. The bottom of the net was pulled shut to form a "purse" so that thousands of pounds of fish could not escape. A large hose was then lowered into the churning school and the fish were vacuumed into the hold of a mother ship.

Photo courtesy of the image collection of the Mariners' Museum, Newport News, VA

To make the back-breaking work go easier, the men sang what were called "chanteys" to coordinate their movements. A leader sang out the first line of the song alone, to be answered with another line sung in harmony by the rest of the crew. The idea was that the harmony synchronized the men and their effort on the same chord at the same time. Songs were borrowed from various sources, including hymns and gospel songs, and blues and barbershop quartet songs, and were often improvised. In 1989 a group of retired black fishermen called the Menhaden Chanteymen recorded a dozen traditional work songs of the coastal Carolina menhaden fishery, titled "Won't You Help Raise 'em", and received the North Carolina Folk Heritage Award. As of May 2012, purse seining was banned in North Carolina waters, but the memory will live on through its music.

Figure 29: *Northern mummichog (Fundulus heteroclitus)*
Illustration courtesy of the Calvert Marine Museum

The mummichog is a stout-bodied little fish, ranging from the Gulf of St. Lawrence to northeastern Florida and growing to about five inches in length. The top of the head is flat between the eyes and the snout is blunt (see fig. 29). The mouth is at the tip of the snout and is so small that it does not extend back to the eye. Out of breeding season the males are dark greenish or steel blue above with white and yellow spots, and marked on the sides with narrow irregular silvery vertical bars, or mottlings, made up of a series of dots. The belly is white, pale yellow, or orange, and the dorsal, anal, and caudal fins are dark green or dusky with pale mottlings. At spawning time, the pigmentation of the male is generally intensified, the back and upper sides darkening almost to black, while the yellow of the belly becomes more brilliant and the body generally takes on steel-blue reflections. The females are larger than the males, uniform olive to bottle green, darker above, lighter below, without definite markings though their sides often show faint and indefinite crossbars of a deeper tone of the same hue. They are omnivores and scavengers, feeding in salt marshes on plankton, mollusks, crustaceans, mosquito larvae, small live fishes, and dead fish. Mummichogs tolerate freshwater well, but normally inhabit shallow marine and brackish estuarine environments, spawning in the marshes in spring and summer. During extreme cold they burrow into the bottoms of the deeper holes or creeks, sometimes six or eight inches deep in the mud.

A species of killifish, mummichogs are otherwise known as "mud minnows", and are very resilient in low oxygen conditions. If trapped in small pools that become dry they again retreat into to the mud where they can absorb oxygen until the pool is re-flooded, so it is not even necessary to keep them in water. For a handy, easily portable live bait container, place some ice in the bottom of a six to eight-quart cooler, and lay several layers of folded newspaper over the ice. The minnows will stay lively on top of the newspaper for over twenty-four hours if kept out of the sun, remaining cool and comfortable while absorbing oxygen and moisture from the damp newspaper.

Mud minnows are easily caught in small creeks and ditches with a minnow trap baited with many different things such as bread, pet food, and hot dogs. While not as prevalent as mullets and menhaden in the western Pamlico, they are a highly desirable live baitfish, being extremely robust and durable on the hook. Whether hooked through the lips or the back they will tolerate being dragged along the bottom from a drifting boat, worked with a Carolina rig, or free swimming below a float. It is not unusual for them to survive successive hook ups with target species or even mauling by crabs.

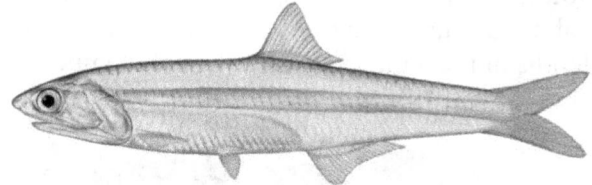

Figure 30: Glass minnow (Anchoa michilli)
Courtesy of Diane Rome Peebles

Glass minnows are anchovies, very similar to the anchovies eaten on pizza. Their range is from Maine throughout the Gulf coast. Very common in shallow marine and brackish waters, they are abundant in bays and estuaries, tolerating a wide range of salinity from fresh to fully saline. Maximum length for glass minnow is about four inches, with a large mouth below the snout. The coloring is silvery transparent, with a broad silver stripe down the side (see fig. 30). They feed on a variety of tiny shrimp, crustaceans, mollusks, and fish. Spawning occurs in spring and summer on the Atlantic coast.

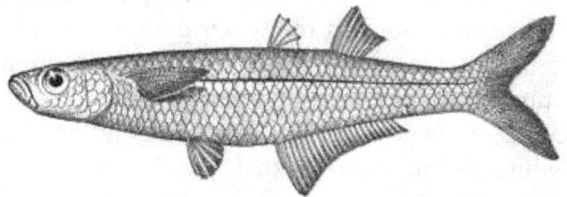

Figure 31: Atlantic silverside (Menidia menidia)

The Atlantic silverside is a long, slender, and thin-bodied fish with two dorsal fins, translucent gray green above, a rounded white belly, and large scales with smooth margins (see fig. 31). They have a short head with large eyes, a small oblique mouth, grow to a length of five inches, and are sometimes called "shiners". The top of the head, nose, and chin are dusky gray. Along each side is a distinct silver band outlined by a narrow black stripe. Silversides resemble glass minnows, differing mainly by a smaller mouth. It is an omnivorous fish which feeds on small plankton, crustaceans, shrimp, young squid, worms, and even insects. The silverside is commonly found in fresh and brackish estuarine waters, swimming among the submerged grasses a few feet from shore, but will descend to greater depths in the winter to avoid the cold temperatures.

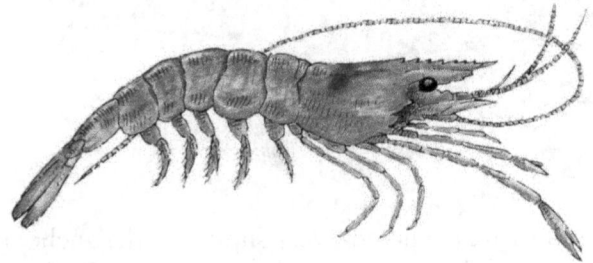

Figure 32: Common grass shrimp (Palaemonetes pugio)
Illustration courtesy of the Calvert Marine Museum

The common grass shrimp lives in shallow waters among grass beds or on the marsh bottom among submerged plant matter in estuaries all along the Atlantic and Gulf coasts. There it swims or crawls, foraging for tiny worms and invertebrates, algae, and decaying plant debris. By breaking down plant debris into tiny particles that are suspended in the water column, it provides a rich food source for smaller organisms. Nearly transparent, it grows to a maximum length of one and a half inches over a lifespan of six to thirteen months (see fig. 32). Grass shrimp are a major food source for white perch, small baitfish, and crabs, thus playing an important role in the food chain. They are present in the Pamlico all year around, usually in shallow water, but may temporarily migrate to deeper water to avoid seasonal temperature extremes. They are pollution tolerant, well adapted to a wide range of salinity and dissolved oxygen, and therefore are an important indicator of overall water quality. To catch them, work a fine mesh dip net along the edge of a marsh or in a shallow grass bed. Then store them in a cool, moist container.

Figure 33: American eel (Anguilla rostrate)

The American eel is found in the Atlantic Ocean from Greenland to Brazil. A slimy mucous layer covers its tiny scales along its slender body. A long dorsal fin runs from the middle of its back and continues ventrally along its belly. It does not have pelvic fins, but small pectoral fins are located behind the gills in the lateral midline. The back ranges from olive-green to brown, is greenish-yellow on the sides, and light gray or white on the belly (see fig. 33).

All American eels are spawned and hatched from eggs into larvae, in the Sargasso Sea near Bermuda. The larvae are then transported by ocean currents to the Atlantic coasts of North and South America. Juvenile eels arrive on the coast as colorless "glass eels" in great numbers, but time of arrival can vary greatly throughout the year. Glass eels develop into pigmented "elvers" that subsequently grow into "yellow eels" resembling adults in size and colored yellow or green. Yellow eels migrate upstream over a broad period from January through October, depending on latitude. Some will reach the extreme upper reaches of the rivers while others may stay behind in brackish waters. Amazingly, the eel is able to absorb oxygen through its skin, as well as gills, and can even travel over land to reach isolated bodies of water, including freshwater lakes and ponds.

Eels reach sexual differentiation at about eight to ten inches long and become male or female, depending on the density of eels in the area. Generally, the yellow eels live in estuaries and freshwater streams for four to ten years before reaching sexual maturity, although some may not mature until over twenty years of age. Females grow the largest, up to five feet, and males reach a maximum length of about three feet. After as few as three years, or for females as many as forty years living in fresh or brackish waters, the eel will reach sexual maturity. At that point the eel becomes more silvery in color, the eyes and pectoral fins are more prominent, and the eel is known as a "silver eel". After reaching sexual maturity the adult eel ceases feeding and begins its journey back to the spawning ground in the Sargasso Sea, where it is thought to die after spawning. The life span for most American eels is fifteen to twenty years, but it may live for more than fifty years in the wild.

Eels are most active at night, swimming and eating small fish, shrimps, and crabs. They have small teeth and relatively weak jaws, so they jerk or pull on food that cannot be eaten whole or easily broken into smaller portions. Holding on with their mouths, adult eels will spin their bodies to break apart food.

Eels can be caught in a plain minnow trap, which they will enter to feed on trapped minnows and grass shrimp, or to steal the bait. However, they are expert escape artists and will typically get out within a few hours. Commercial eel pots of several designs that prevent escape can be purchased. An infinite number of bait choices will lure eels into a trap, including chicken livers and parts, turkey necks, cut bait fish, and crushed crabs. Since eels are primarily night feeders, the best time to set traps is in the evening and collect them the following morning.

The American Eel is a significant prey species throughout its life stages for many fish, mammals, water snakes, and fish-eating birds. It is considered a delicacy in Asian markets, its flesh white, firm, and mild. In the Carolinas, small yellow eels are harvested for highly effective bait to catch striped bass, but can be expensive. A live, wriggling eel can be very difficult to hold and control with bare hands. It is best to store them chilled on ice, which renders them lethargic, and to handle them with a dry rag. Hook the eel through its lower jaw and out one eye, which will hold on the hook, and keep it alive and moving. In shallow water, hooks can be tied onto a heavy monofilament or fluorocarbon leader several feet in length connected to the main line with a barrel swivel. In deep water, a slip sinker should be added above the barrel swivel as a Carolina Rig (see Chapter 3) or crimped into place, similar to a drum rig (see Chapter 4).

"I believe a leaf of grass is no less
than the journey-work of the stars."
—WALT WHITMAN

CHAPTER 12
SUBMERGED AQUATIC VEGETATION

❖ ❖ ❖

Submerged aquatic vegetation (SAV), also called seagrass or sea weed, consists of vascular plants that are rooted in the bottom sediments. Habitat includes marine, estuarine, and riverine environments. Although sometimes extending to the surface of the water, these plants are generally submerged. Their importance to the overall ecologic health and productivity of the estuary cannot be overstated.

Beds of SAV in the western Pamlico occur in sheltered riverine and estuarine waters where the bottom sediment is loose and unconsolidated. Prevailing currents or wave turbulence must be moderate to minimal. Sufficient sun light must be able to penetrate to the bottom, at least fifteen to twenty-five percent of the light available at the surface. Otherwise photosynthesis is inadequate, reproduction may be inhibited, and growth and survival cannot be sustained. Thus, water clarity and light penetration are the primary factors controlling distribution of SAV. In the Pamlico, seagrass growth is generally limited to depths of below about eight feet, and when water clarity declines the beds in the deeper water are lost first. Even though the western shoreline of the sound is generally less protected from the wind, the reduced currents, low tidal forces, and extensive shallows provide suitable habitat for SAV growth when water clarity and other water quality conditions allow.

SAV beds support numerous complex food chains and are recognized as essential finfish and shellfish habitat. Many species utilize it at some point in their life cycles, either by consuming it as a food source, hunting for prey along the edge of the beds, finding refuge from predators, or for spawning. Included among the finfish relevant to healthy recreational fisheries are prey species such as croaker, spot, mullet, mud minnows, glass minnows, herring, shad, eel, menhaden, and white perch. Striped bass, speckled trout, red drum, and southern flounder, are a few of the higher order predators who rely on SAV as an important resource. Blue crabs and other crustaceans, small invertebrates, various shrimp species, bay scallops, and hard clams are also strongly dependent on SAV beds. Increased quantity and health of SAV are strongly associated with more abundant, diverse fish populations.

Aside from providing critical fish habitat, seagrass beds enhance the water qualities that they and other species in the ecosystem are dependent on. The leaves, stems, and roots oxygenate the surrounding water through photosynthesis. Sediments are filtered, trapped, and removed from the water column by slowing the velocity of waves and current, allowing the sediment to settle on the bottom. There, the roots and bulbs stabilize the sediment and help prevent it from being stirred up again. SAVs moderate erosion on nearby shorelines, by buffering wave energy, further reducing turbidity and helping to maintain marsh edge habitat. Just as agricultural plants take up nitrogen and phosphorous nutrient fertilizers, seagrasses consume them as well, thereby reducing the chance that excess nutrients can result in noxious algal blooms (see chapter 1). All of these processes promote water clarity and improve overall conditions for further SAV growth.

Dredging, filling activities, and infrastructure placement such as marinas and bridges have had great destructive impact on SAV. Shading results in severe loss of light beneath docks. Bottom disturbing commercial fishing gear can destroy or damage SAV. Repeated agitation from boating wakes causes significant detrimental effect to seagrass beds by eroding, destabilizing, and re-suspending the bottom sediments beneath them, and reducing light penetration. Propeller scarring occurs when outboard power boats motor through shallow areas, cutting up the leaves, stems, and roots of SAVs, and churning a narrow trench through the sediment referred to as a 'prop scar'. A 'blow hole' may also be created where boaters attempt to rapidly power off a shallow bottom. Recovery of SAV from mechanically damaged areas may take extensive periods of time, sometimes many years, if at all. Fishermen and other boaters should exercise deliberate care to avoid such damage.

The major cause of SAV loss in the western Pamlico, both direct and indirect, is large-scale nutrient overloading. Turbidity and poor light penetration is chronically aggravated by algal growth associated with high nutrient loads. Excessive growth of algal species that naturally grow on the surface of leaf blades, as well as drifting algae can smother photosynthetic production of oxygen by SAV. Furthermore, the algae consume it during their own respiration, leading to acute and long-term depletion of oxygen levels in the water (see Chapter 1).

SAV habitat in the Western Pamlico is divided into two types of communities: higher salinity estuarine waters in one, and lower salinity to freshwater environments in the other (see Appendix E). The three estuarine species are eelgrass (*Zostera marina*), shoalgrass (*Halodule wrightii*), and widgeon grass (*Ruppia maritima*). Eelgrass is a species of moderate temperature ranges, occurring at the southern limit of its Atlantic coastal range in North Carolina.

Conversely, NC is the northern most extent for shoalgass, a tropical species. Widgeon grass grows most commonly in moderate salinities (15 ppt), but has a wide salinity tolerance and is found in both freshwater and high salinity waters. The convergence of these three SAV species gives North Carolina's estuaries the potential for relatively high coverage of shallow bottoms, and is unique to the state. Low salinity species occurring in the Pamlico include wild celery (*Vallisneria americana*), redhead grass (*Potamogeton perfoliatus*), sago pondweed (*Potamogeton pectinatus*), bushy pondweed (*Najas guadalupensis*), and non-native Eurasian watermilfoil (*Myriophyllum spicatum*).

*"She'll run so shallow the seagulls
can walk out of the way."*

—UNKNOWN
HARKER'S ISLAND FISHERMAN

CHAPTER 13
GETTING THERE
❖ ❖ ❖

O ver time, fishermen of all the great bodies of water on
the globe have crafted boats to meet the specific needs
as demanded by local conditions. Just as in nature, form
follows function. Males are biologically built to be hunter-gatherers.
Female bodies are biologically engineered for nesting, child bearing,
and nurturing. Practical attributes aside, boats and people are much
alike in that beauty is often in the eye of the beholder, at least initially.
The difference is that in a boat it will not take long for blind love
to find sight. A rich boat building tradition that continues to this
day has endowed eastern North Carolinians with vessels equally
useful and aesthetically pleasing. There are three basic categories
upon which variations are predicated.

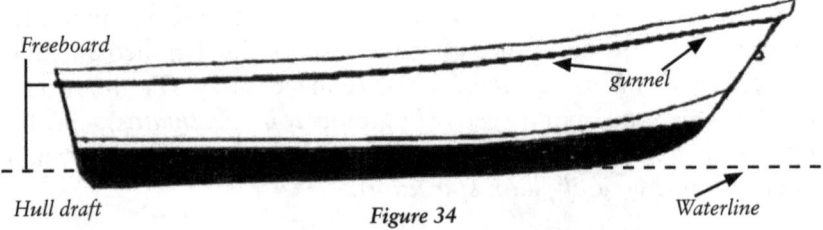

Freeboard

gunnel

Hull draft   **Figure 34**   *Waterline*

In its pure form, the 'skiff" or "skimmer" style boat (see fig.
35), as it is known provincially, features a flat bottom from stern to
bow, with no deadrise (see fig. 36) and no keel. The hull draft (see
fig. 34) is very shallow and displaces a relatively small volume of
water, which translates into less power required to move the boat.

In any age of technology, the implication for energy efficiency is obvious. Cost of construction is minimized and space utilization is maximized by the rectangular line of the gunnels and the sides that rise straight up from the deck. It can be thought of as a floating shallow box, beveled on the bow end. The skiff is a roomy craft, able to venture into the shallows with ease, and serves as a stable fishing platform. However, these boats are not designed to ride smoothly across the blunt vertical chop that the Pamlico is known for in its deeper, unprotected fetches. In fact, skiffs can "beat your teeth right out of your head". This statement should be qualified by the common knowledge that any hull style will pound progressively less as length increases.

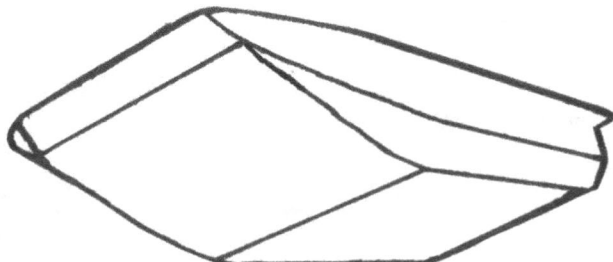

Figure 35: "Skiff" or "Skimmer"

The antithesis of the flat bottom skiff is the deep vee hull (see fig. 36), which enables a boat to split the chop and slice through tall waves in open water, depending on the degree of dead rise. Their typically higher freeboard makes for a safe, drier ride, and minimizes the chance of overwash. The clear disadvantage is that these hulls draft more depth, thus limiting their range in shallow water. The less apparent drawback is that their increased volume of water displacement consequently requires added power to propel. Thirdly, the deep vee is more prone to rocking side to side with shifts in weight. It is unapologetically made for rapidly crossing long expanses of rough seas.

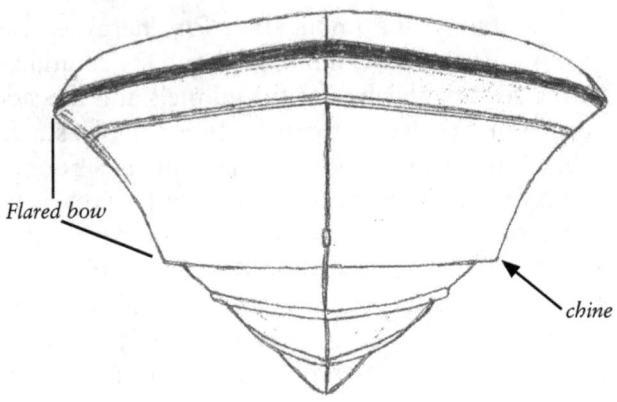

Flared bow

chine

Figure 36: Deep Vee

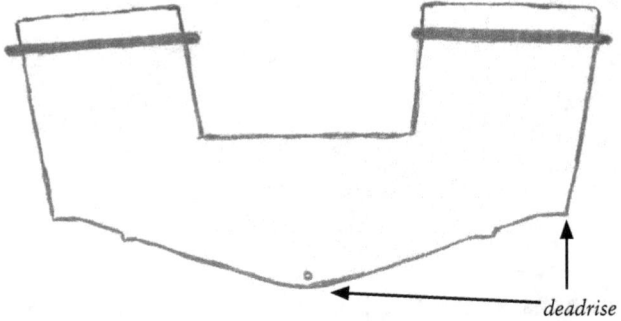

deadrise

Modified vees (see fig. 37) display a similar, but usually less exaggerated sharp deadrise at the bow, and quickly begin to flatten out at about halfway toward the stern, some almost completely. On the majority of factory produced modified vees, the deadrise in the stern is ten to fourteen degrees. An increased ratio of beam-to-length gives the hull stability and allows the boat to draw much less water. While not the smooth ride of a deep vee, a well-designed modified vee can buffer a considerable amount of wave action and still provides access to comparatively shallow areas.

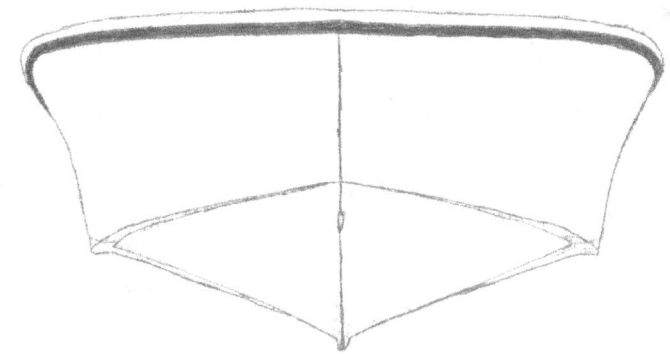

Figure 37: Modified Vee

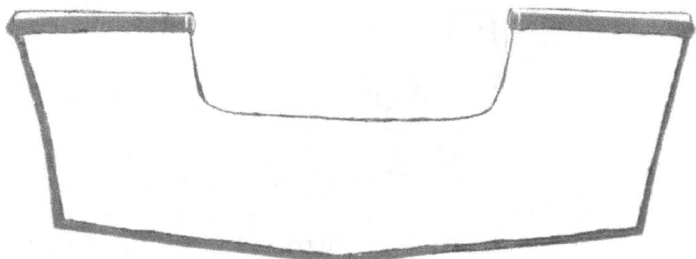

Whether a modified or deep vee hull, the gunnels should rise prominently toward the bow while the sides curve gracefully inward to form the distinctive "Carolina flare". This lovely trait enhances a dry, comfortable ride by deflecting waves, wind, and spray. The perfect multi-purpose boat does not exist for the Pamlico, but some combinations of design come close. Anglers would be wise to adopt the hull configuration that most closely matches their fishing interests and financial comfort zone.

*"When we were learning to fish big fish together we used
to be excited and rude and sarcastic. We both used to be
terrible. We used to suffer and act as though everybody
was against us. That's the natural way to be. The other's
discipline or good sense when you learn. We started to be
polite because we found we couldn't catch big fish being rude
and excited. And if we did, it wasn't any fun. We were both
really awful though; excited and sore and misunderstood and
it wasn't any fun. So now we always fight them politely. We
talked it over and decided we'd be polite no matter what."*
–FROM *ISLANDS IN THE STREAM*,
BY EARNEST HEMINGWAY

AFTERWORD
❖ ❖ ❖

The Pamlico Sound, its sub-estuaries, rivers, and innumerable
creeks are a treasure trove of biodiversity. *A New Voyage
to Carolina*, written by John Lawson in the early eighteenth
century, and the drawings of John White in the late sixteenth century
strongly suggest that the productivity of our rivers and sounds
is only a shadow of what it once was. Other isolated fragments
of historical documentation by elderly fishermen and fishermen's
journal accounts from the late 1800s describe extensive meadows of
SAV along the mainland side of the sounds, where it is now depleted
or absent. In 1889, Lieutenant Francis Winslow of the U.S. Navy
published a survey of oysters and potential oyster habitat in North
Carolina's sounds. Public areas, vulnerable to hand harvest methods,
were felt to be in degraded condition, even at that time. Still, he was
able to identify over 8,000 acres of natural oyster beds, much of
which was located in the middle and western portions of the sounds.
The rich cultural tradition of harvesting and consuming herring
from immense schools each spring has dramatically dissipated.

Indians Fishing by John White (circa 1585)

An accurate, comprehensive description of these waters in their pristine condition is lacking, and so there is no basis for reference. Each generation of North Carolinians has a different expectation of what is natural, because they each experience an increasingly altered ecological system. Declining water quality and degradation of habitat have been directly attributed to multiple human activities. Point and non-point sources of industrial, agricultural, municipal, and residential pollution have all been identified as important factors. Poorly planned flood plain and shore-line development, upstream channelization, and destruction of forested riparian buffers and wetlands have resulted in a significant loss of the vital mechanisms by which surface waters cleanse themselves. Unsustainable commercial and recreational fishing pressure for highly desired species, including controversial methods of harvest, has been implicated for further decimating already stressed resources. To complicate matters more, the affected components of the Pamlico estuarine system are known to be very complex in their interactions with each other, and are not well understood in many cases.

The challenge in managing any natural resource is to allow some measure of safeguard for uncertainties to insure the future health of the resource. In this respect, proper management is difficult because those profiting from a public resource are typically not required to prove their actions cause no harm. Management often focuses on avoiding short-term economic losses, sometimes failing to recognize and prevent severe long-term damage. In the discussion of "property rights", the property rights of the public are usually not given adequate consideration. When a source of pollution degrades the quality of public trust waters downstream, it may unfairly detract from a potentially more valuable array of economic activity and recreation available to everyone, thus infringing on the property rights of the public. The only available recourse for society to protect a resource may be to somehow prove clearly tangible, unacceptable consequences of the activity in question.

Given the complexity and magnitude of reasons for ecologic damage, it is difficult to imagine the Pamlico restored to its pre-colonial state, and would almost certainly be an exercise in futility to attempt such a feat. In nature, niches will continually be created and destroyed over time, even when free from human impact. Free market systems are much like ecologic systems. Where there is a niche someone will fill it.

The role of government should not be to tell business or industry how to reach goals, but it is certainly appropriate for government to set goals for the good of all. Necessity has always been the mother of invention. Undoubtedly, the system will survive in some form for the foreseeable future, but the citizens of North Carolina hold the keys to what it will look like. When the repressed potential of basic natural processes is given a chance, renewal of healthy and productive ecosystems will normally follow, albeit often different than a historical ideal. The opportunity to live in a more mature relationship with our environment is before us each day. Responsibility, stewardship, and prudence as individuals and as a society demand that we do so.

Appendix A
SHORELINE VEGETATION
❖ ❖ ❖

Smooth cordgrass or saltmarsh cordgrass
Spartina alterniflora

Smooth Cordgrass is a perennial deciduous grass which is the dominant wetland plant of the salt and brackish marshes of Atlantic coast estuaries. It is a hardy, salt tolerant plant that is able to withstand saltwater flooding and battering by waves, making it valuable for erosion control and sediment trapping. A nursery for finfish, crabs, and shellfish, its roots and shoots are a food source for waterfowl and small mammals. Its prolific seasonal growth and decay contributes large amounts of decomposing plant matter, a major component of the estuarine food web. Height ranges from two to seven feet in different zones of the marsh. Generally, the tall form occurs along the stream banks, followed by an intermediate form moving landward, and a more stunted form at the marsh interior.

Saltmeadow hay
Spartina patens

Saltmeadow hay is a fine, wiry grass that grows in dense patches often associated with smooth cordgrass, but is less tolerant of the salt and low oxygen conditions, and is typically seen further up in the less flooded marsh zones. One to two feet is the usual height, although it may grow as long as five feet. The base of the stem is weak, making it prone to bend when stressed by winds or flooding, which gives it a matted cowlick or swirling appearance. It also colonizes sand dunes, grasslands, sand flats, and scrublands near the sea. In colonial times it served as an important source of fodder and bedding for farm animals along the coast. Like smooth cordgrass it functions as a pollution filter and reduces shoreline erosion.

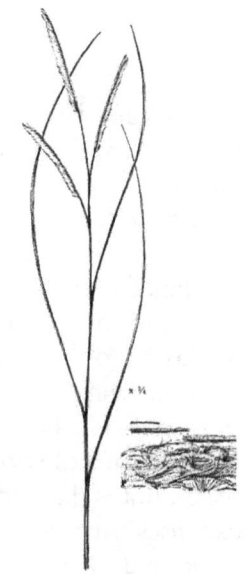

Big cordgrass
Spartina cynosuroides

Big cordgrass is the largest and least salt tolerant of the Spartina marsh grasses, easily attaining heights of twelve feet or more in brackish to nearly freshwater marshes, and is seldom found in high saline marshes. It grows in thick stands along the rivers and creeks of the western Pamlico and often forms a tall border in the transition zone between marsh and upland. The dense stands provide food and shelter for wildlife, including geese that eat the large roots and muskrats who use the stems for lodge construction. It is rivaled only by smooth cordgrass in its export of decaying plant

material to the estuarine food web. When broken off and stood in a few derelict crab pots, it makes a handy and effective duck blind.

Black needle rush
Juncus roemerianus

Black needle rush is a stiff, leafless rush that grows in dense stands of nearly uniform heights of two to five feet. The stems are actually leaves that are rounded tightly to form very sharp-pointed stems. The leaves combined with its grayish-green to blackish hues give this plant its name. It occurs in a variety of salt and brackish settings, often growing at or below the water line. In the western Pamlico it may be found in isolated patches within high salinity marsh zones, but is the dominant species in broad expanses at the headwaters of creeks, associated with lower salinity water and muddy bottom sediment.

APPENDIX B
ESSENTIAL KNOTS
❖ ❖ ❖

Bimini Twist—for making an end loop
Illustration © Leadertec Ltd., England

Step 1: Make a loop and twist the line at least twenty times. It may be necessary to attach the double to something.

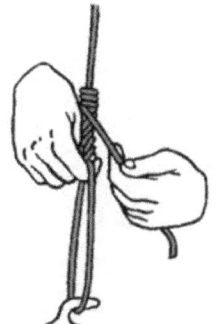

Step 2: Keeping tension on the main line to the reel, relax the tag end slightly and let it run down over the original twist.

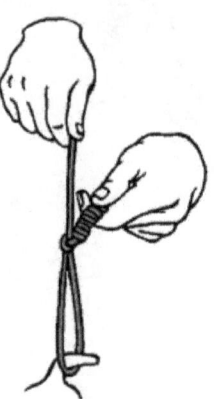

Step 3: When the twists are completely wrapped, make a half-hitch around the right leg of the loop and pull tight.

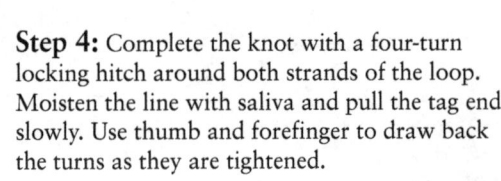

Step 4: Complete the knot with a four-turn locking hitch around both strands of the loop. Moisten the line with saliva and pull the tag end slowly. Use thumb and forefinger to draw back the turns as they are tightened.

Blood Knot—for joining two lines
Illustration by Neil Kenney, from *Practical Fishing Knots*, 1972

Step 1:

Step 2:

Step 3:

PULL   PULL

Step 4:

Improved Blood Knot—for joining lines of greatly different diameter
Illustration by Neil Kenney, from *Practical Fishing Knots*, 1972

Step 1:

Step 2:

Step 3:

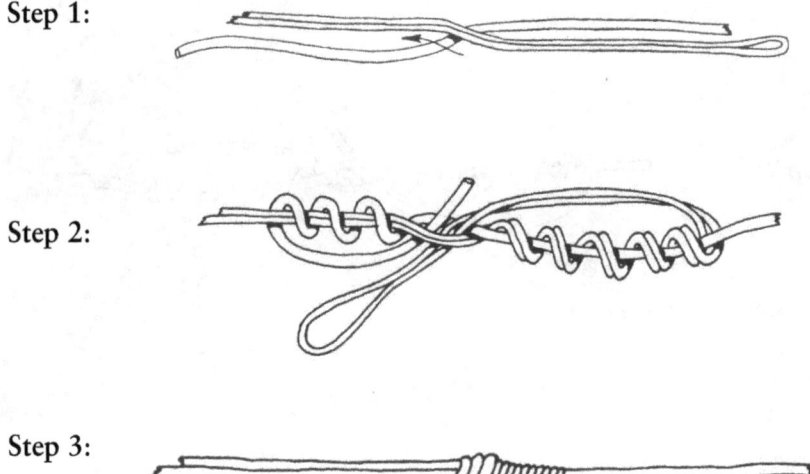

Clinch Knot—for tying line to terminal tackle
Illustration by Geoff Wilson,
© *Encyclopedia of Fishing Knots and Rigs*

Step 1: Thread the eye of the hook with the line.

Step 2: Make an extra loop.

Step 3: Wrap the tag around the main line from 3 to 5 times. The heavier the line used, the fewer the number of wraps. The lighter the line, the more wraps.

Step 4: Pass the tag back through the first two wraps before pullingthe knot tight.

Double Overhand Loop (or Surgeon's Loop)
—a quick and easy way to tie an end loop
Illustration by Geoff Wilson,
© *Encyclopedia of Fishing Knots and Rigs*

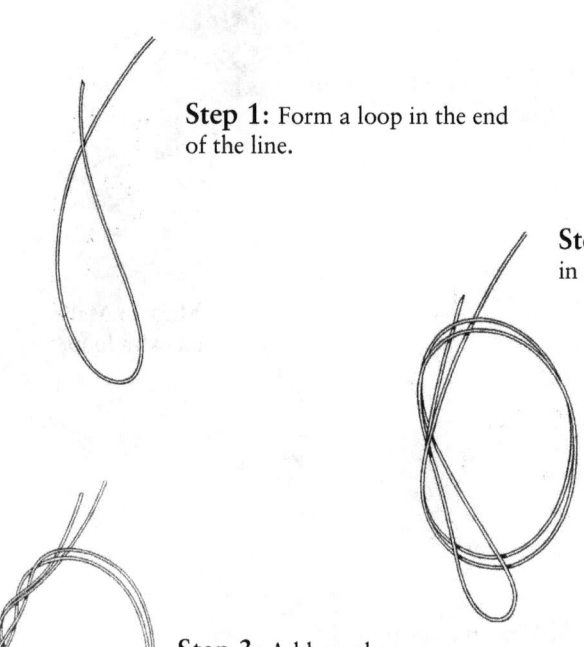

Step 1: Form a loop in the end of the line.

Step 2: Tie the loop in an overhand knot.

Step 3: Add another wrap to the knot.

Step 4: Pass the tag back through the first two wraps before pulling the knot tight.

Dropper Loop—can be tied anywhere along a length of line for attachment of a hook or leader
Illustration by Geoff Wilson,
© *Encyclopedia of Fishing Knots and Rigs*

Step 1: Make a generous loop in the line where the dropper is to be tied, then pull out a section of the loop so that it crosses over the main line at one side forming a second smaller loop.

Step 2: Begin twisting the smaller loop, alternating the twisting and holding between hands.

Step 3: Make 4 to 6 complete twists, then thread the larger loop through the smaller loop.

Step 4: Put the larger loop around a peg or the like and gently pull both sides of the knot until it pulls up neatly.

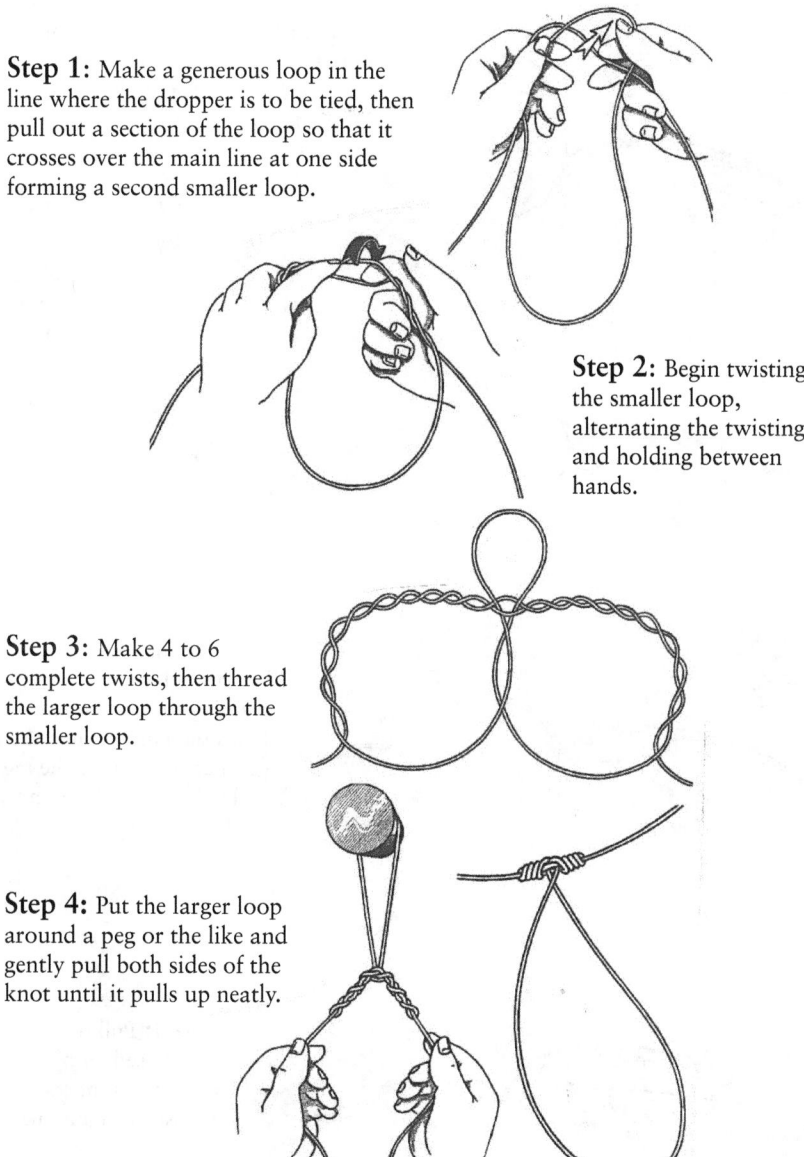

Perfection Loop—for attaching a lure to a leader loop, to allow freedom of movement
Illustration by Geoff Wilson,
© *Encyclopedia of Fishing Knots and Rigs*

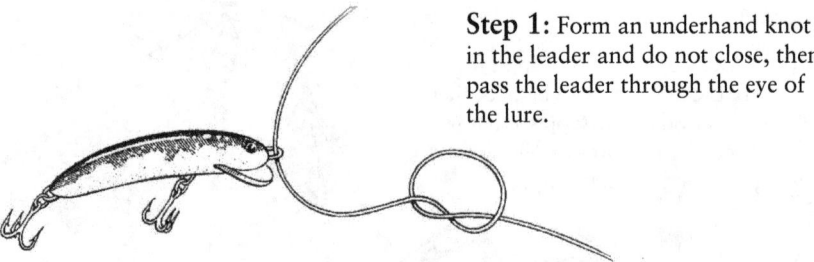

Step 1: Form an underhand knot in the leader and do not close, then pass the leader through the eye of the lure.

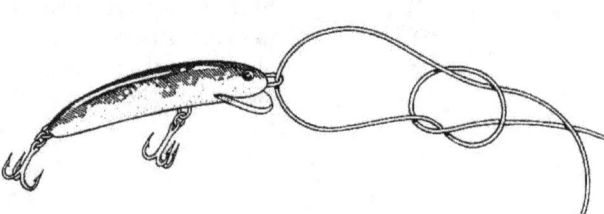

Step 2: Thread the tag end back through the underhand knot.

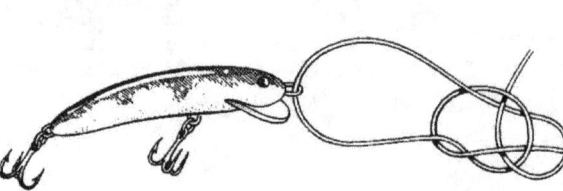

Step 3: Bring the tag end over the main line, up through the crossover forming the underneath knot, then up through the gap between where the tag end was passed through the knot in step 2.

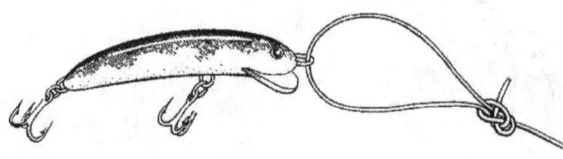

Step 4: Pull the knot closed with pressure on the loop against the main line.

Spider Hitch—for making an end loop or double line
Illustration © Leadertec Ltd., England

Step 1: Double over the line and form a reverse loop.

Step 2: Hold the reverse loop between thumb and forefinger.

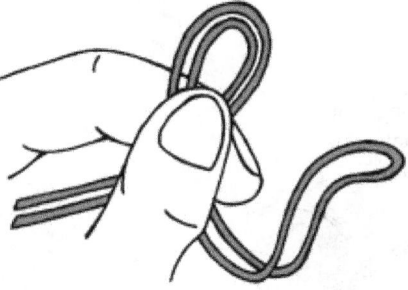

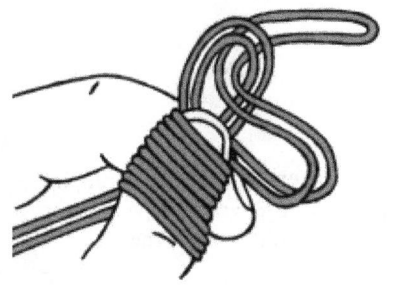

Step 3: Wrap the doubled line around the thumb and the reversed loop five times, then pass the end of the double line through the reverse loop. Slowly pull on the double line allowing the loops to unwind off the thumb.

Step 4: Moisten with saliva and pull evenly on all four ends to tighten.

Common Snell Knot—for hooks with up or down turned eyes
Illustration by Geoff Wilson,
© *Encyclopedia of Fishing Knots and Rigs*

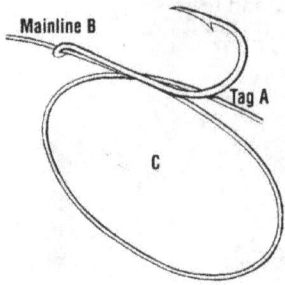

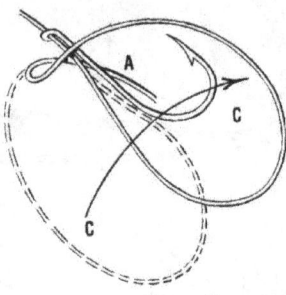

Step 1: Thread the line through the hook and make this configuration.

Step 2: Pull loop C over to form loop D, and begin wrapping loop C around the shank and tag A.

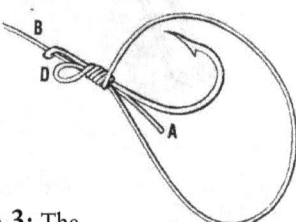

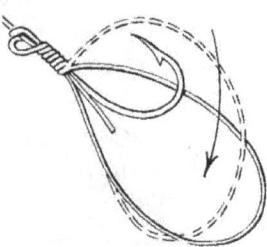

Step 3: The snell should begin looking something like this.

Step 4: Continue wrapping for 5-8 wraps, depending on the thickness of the line.

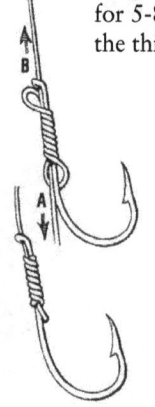

Step 5: Pull on main line B against tag A until the knot is formed on the shank.

Uni-knot—used for attaching tackle to the end of a line
Illustration by Geoff Wilson,
© *Encyclopedia of Fishing Knots and Rigs*

Step 1: Thread the eye of the hook with the line so that the hook is suspended on a loop.

Step 2: Encircle the main line with the tag end so that another loop is formed.

Step 3: Wrap the double strand inside the loop with the tag end.

Step 4: Make four wraps in all, leaving the tag end protruding from the loop.

Step 5: Close the knot but do not pull it tight yet.

Step 6: Slide the knot down onto the eye of the hook, pull it tight, and trim the tag.

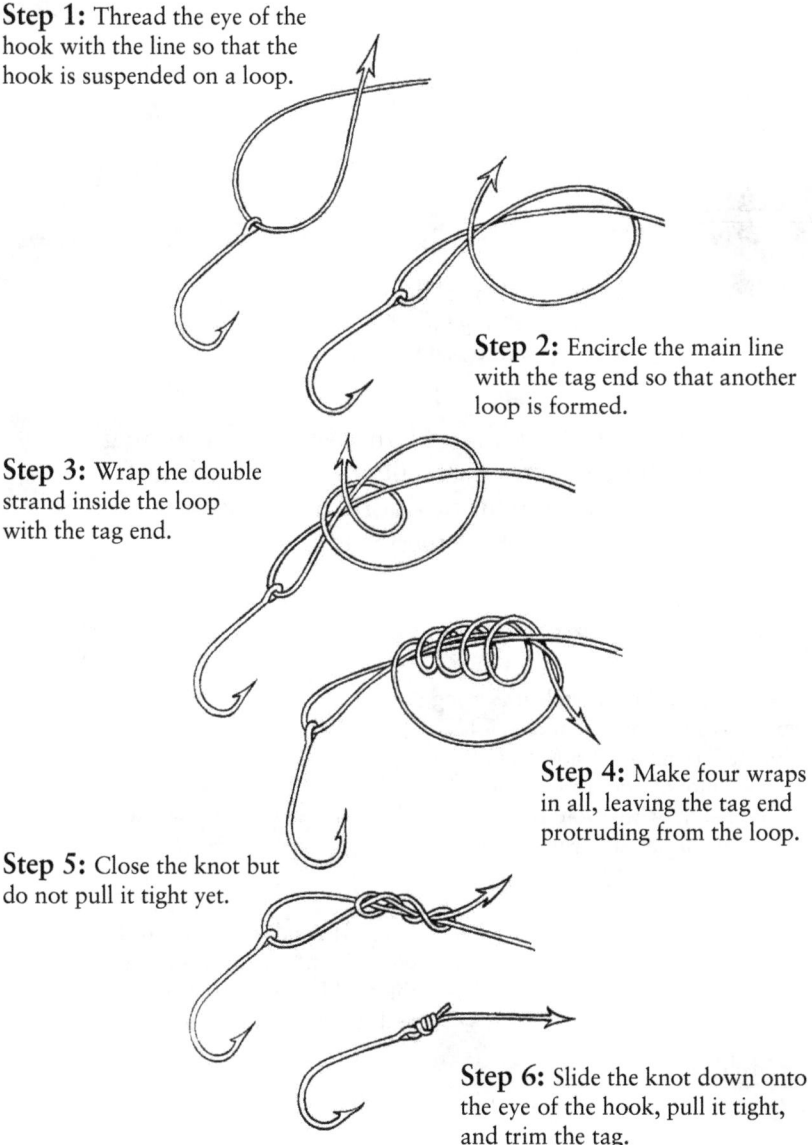

Double Uni-knot—for joining two lines
© David Hall, illustrator

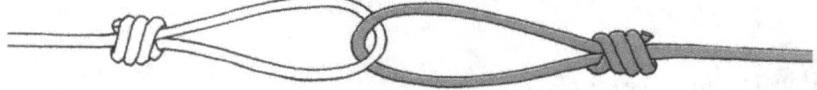

Step 1: Form a uni-knot loop, pass the tag end of the second line through the loop, and tie a uni-knot loop in the second line.

Step 2: Pull on both main lines, joining the two lines together. Pull firmly on each tag end to seat the knots snugly.

Yucatan Knot (aka No Name Knot)—for joining two lines together, excellent for joining braid to monofilament or fluorocarbon leaders
Illustration © Leadertec Ltd., England

Step 1: Make a short double line using a Bimini twist or a Spider hitch. Hold the double line and the leader parallel. If joining a monoleader to superbraid make the Bimini with 30-40 turns instead of the usual 20 turns.

Step 2: Wrap the double line four times around the leader (15 times for superbraid).

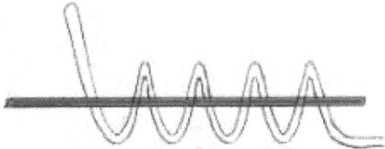

Step 3: Bend the end of the leader back on itself and pass it through the end of the double line. Lubricate with saliva and carefully pull tight.

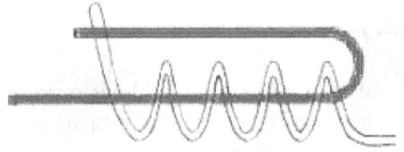

Palomar Knot—a simple means of tying hooks at the end of a line, or along a line as is the case when rigging a drop-shot for soft plastics
Illustration by Geoff Wilson,
© *Encyclopedia of Fishing Knots and Rigs*

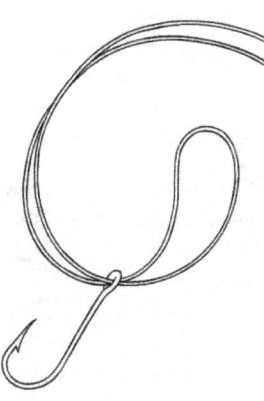

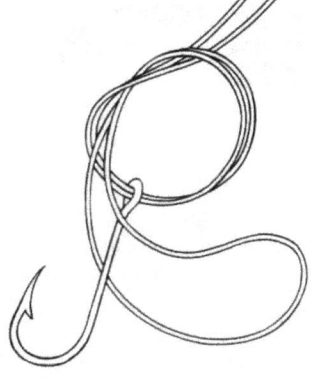

Step 1: Double the main line to form a loop and thread it through the eye of the hook.

Step 2: Isolate the hook on the doubled line by tying an overhand knot over the eye and pass the hook through the loop.

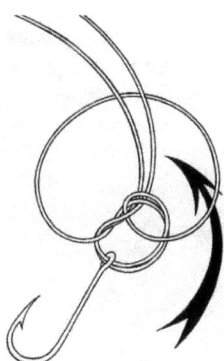

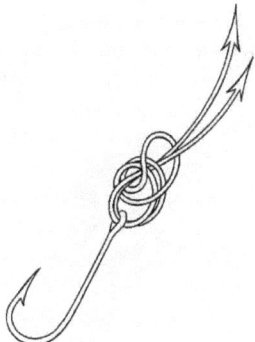

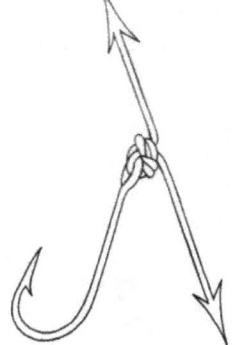

Step 3: Bend the loop back against the doubled line.

Step 4: Close the knot by pulling on the doubled strand. You can trim the tag.

Step 5: Or leave the tag strand intact for a drop shot rig.

Albright Knot—for joining two lines together, excellent for joining braid to a monofilament or fluorocarbon leader
Illustration by Geoff Wilson,
© *Encyclopedia of Fishing Knots and Rigs*

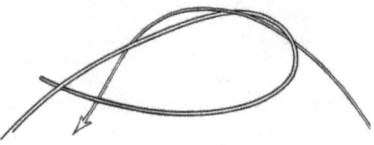

Step 1: Double the desired length of heavier monofilament or fluorocarbon leader, and thread the lighter line of braid through and around the loop.

Step 2: Continue wrapping down the loop in the heavier line with the lighter line.

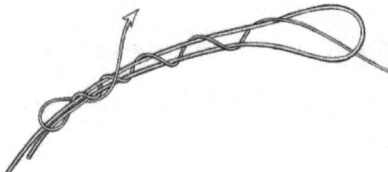

Step 3: Make five wraps down the loop, then begin wrapping in the other direction, back over the first wraps.

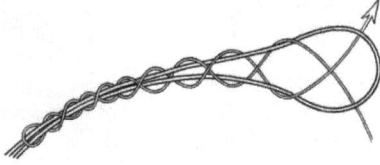

Step 4: Complete fivee wraps in each direction and thread the tag back through the loop alongside the main line.

Step 5: Partially close the knot with gentle pressure on the main line and tag of both lines.

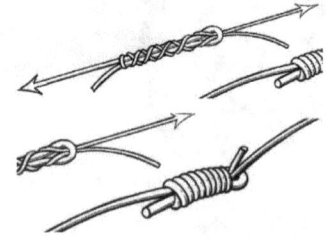

Steps 6 & 7: When the knot begins to tighten, let the tag of both lines go. Then tighten with firm pressure on both main lines. Close the knot and trim the tags.

Appendix C
Basic Lures

Lead head jigs are made in many shapes, colors, and sizes

The classic combination of lead head
jig skirted with curly tailed grub

Plain baitfish

Square paddle tail

Paddle tail shad

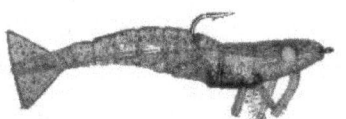

Shrimp with embedded hook

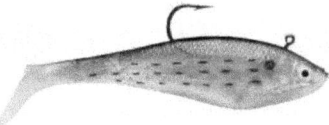

Modern holographic shad with
pre-embedded hook and weight

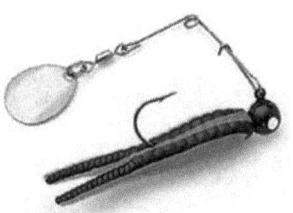

Traditional spinner bait

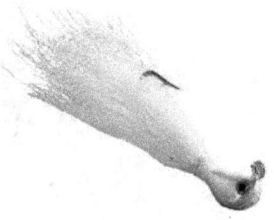

Bucktail lead head

Conventional casting
or trolling spoon

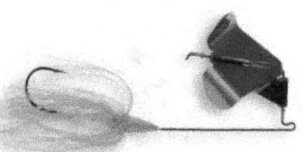

Buzzbait

Sinking or floating
hard plastic plug

Lipped diving plug

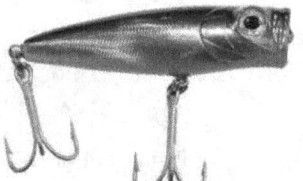

Basic surface plug

Surface popper

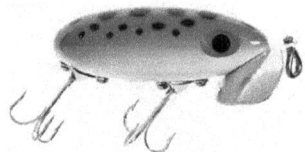

Jittering surface plug

APPENDIX D
HOOK TYPES
❖ ❖ ❖

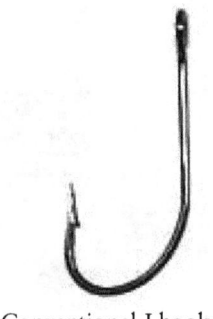

Conventional J hook

Live bait hook

Circle hook

Octopus circle hook with
bent eye for snelling

HIGH AND LOW SALINITY GRASSES

❖ ❖ ❖

High Salinity Grasses

Eelgrass grows in fine muds, silts, and loose sands in high salinity waters. It is able to withstand high energy wave action and currents.

Eelgrass (Zostera marina)

Courtesy of the
Chesapeake Bay Program

Widgeon Grass
(Ruppia maritima)

Courtesy of the
Chesapeake Bay Program

Widgeon grass tolerates a wide range of salinity from slightly brackish to moderately brackish and high salinity. While more common in shallow water on sandy sediments, it is also found on soft, muddy bottoms, in deeper water with eelgrass. High wave action is damaging to its slender stems and leaves.

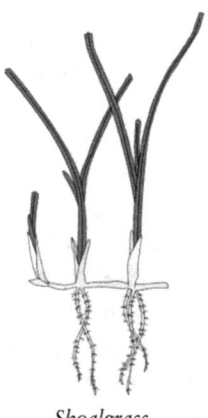

Forming dense beds and able to thrive in very shallow water, shoalgrass can survive drying out for short periods of time once it is rooted, but is sensitive to changing estuarine conditions.

Shoalgrass
(Halodule wrightii)

Courtesy of the University
of Maryland Center for
Environmental Sciences

Low Salinity Grasses

Bushy pondweed is usually present in small freshwater streams, and can also tolerate slightly brackish waters. It prefers sandy sediments, but is sometimes found in muddy areas. It requires less light than other SAV species.

Bushy pondweed
(Najas guadalupensis)

Courtesy of the University
of Maryland Center for
Environmental Sciences

Like bushy pondweed, wild celery is primarily a freshwater species that occasionally grows in moderately brackish waters, in coarse silt to slightly sandy bottoms. It can withstand murky waters and high nutrient levels, as well as some wave action and current. The canvasback duck, *Athya vallisneria*, is so named in recognition of wild celery as the duck's favored food staple during the winter months.

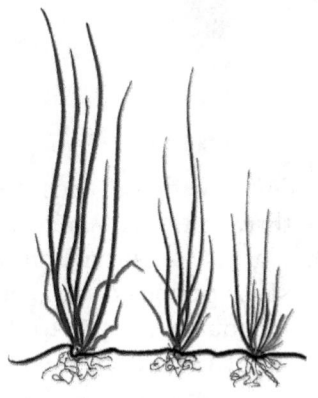

Wild celery (Vallisneria americana)

Courtesy of the
Chesapeake Bay Program

Sago pondweed
(Potamogeton pectinatus)

Courtesy of the
Chesapeake Bay Program

Sago pondweed is found in fresh to moderately brackish waters and is associated with silt or mud sediments. It is capable of enduring stronger currents and greater wave energy than most other seagrasses.

Redhead grass occurs in fresh to moderately brackish salinities, and grows best on firm, muddy bottoms in quiet waters with slow moving currents.

Redhead grass
(Patomogeton perfoliatus)

A non-native invasive species, Eurasian watermilfoil inhabits fresh to moderately brackish waters on soft to sandy mud bottoms, in slow moving streams or protected areas. It is not tolerant of strong currents or wave action. In early spring its over-wintering lower stems provide cover for juvenile fish before other SAV species begin their seasonal growth.

Eurasian watermilfoil
(Myrophyllum spicatum)

Courtesy of the
Chesapeake Bay Program

ABOUT THE AUTHOR

❖ ❖ ❖

Captain Peter Boettger grew up fishing on Maryland's Eastern Shore. In 1985, he completed Physician's Assistant training at Duke University Medical Center and in 2002 he earned an MS in Biology at East Carolina University. Peter has been fishing the Pamlico since moving to Greenville, NC in 1987. He has remained involved in local environmental activism since that time, and is now owner/operator of Machapunga Ecotours (**www.machatours.com**).

CPSIA information can be obtained
at www.ICGtesting.com
Printed in the USA
LVHW052033221121
704136LV00014B/1951